YORKSHIRE
PEOPLE & COAL

Frickley Branch NUM march through Hyde Park, 21 October 1992. In its heyday in the 1930s the colliery employed 4,000 men and boys, and at its closure on 26 November 1993, only 735 men.

Describing the atmosphere at Sharlston on 13 October 1992, Marianne McDonald wrote in the *Yorkshire Post* the following day, 'The dull calm which precedes the executioner's blow hung over Sharlston's rows of uneven pit terraces yesterday, over the scrubby hedges, the ugly pylons, the flat winter fields and the pit itself. That afternoon 750 men would hear that they had lost their jobs – for many the last they would have along with the camaraderie of the work and the family tradition of mining Sharlston pit.' Sharlston miners are pictured with their banner in preparation for a march through Wakefield on 27 November 1992.

YORKSHIRE
PEOPLE & COAL

FROM THE **YORKSHIRE POST** PICTURE ARCHIVES

PETER TUFFREY

AMBERLEY

One of the coaches carrying strike-breaking miners into work at Kellingley colliery, Knottingley, on 16 November 1984.

First published 2012

Amberley Publishing
The Hill, Stroud
Gloucestershire, GL5 4EP

www.amberleybooks.com

British Library Cataloguing in Publication Data.
A catalogue record for this book is available from the British Library.

ISBN 978 1 4456 0516 6

Typesetting and Origination by Amberley Publishing.
Printed in Great Britain.

Contents

Members of the Denby Grange NUM are pictured in November 1991 presenting their banner to the Yorkshire Mining Museum at Caphouse colliery following the closure of their colliery earlier in that year. Made in 1987, the red-and-gold banner replaced the original one which was torn in half by a gale during a march. Ms Tina Lewis, marketing manager at the museum, said, 'We have temporarily loaned the banner before on occasions, but we are delighted to have the banner as a permanent feature for all the visitors to see.'

Acknowledgements

I am grateful for assistance from the following people: Paul Bolton, Peter Charlton, David Clay, David Douglass, Fred Gething, Keith Hampshire, Paul License, Hugh Parkin Jane Salt.

Special thanks to my son Tristam who, as always, provided invaluable support and practical assistance behind the scenes.

Introduction

This is the third book to feature photographs from the *Yorkshire Post* picture archives. The two previous titles were *Yorkshire People & Railways* and *Yorkshire People at Work*. In this present volume it is interesting to note that east, west, north and south Yorkshire have all been involved with coal mining, some dating back to very early times. But the wealth of pictures held in the *Yorkshire Post* archives mainly dates from the 1960s to the present day, though there are a number of original prints and copy prints dating from much earlier and a mixture is included here. Most aspects of colliery life are depicted and perhaps not surprisingly several categories dominate throughout: disasters, strikes and closures.

The disasters bring into sharp focus the perils that each miner faced when descending the shaft for an honest day's pay. The scale of the Oaks colliery disaster in 1866 where two explosions killed 361 men and boys seems incomprehensible today. This is particularly brought into focus when realising the lack of medical facilities and experience available at the time, the primitive rescue resources available and the non-existent social network of support for the families of those killed.

Findings from the Lofthouse and Houghton Main disasters proved how costly human errors or ignoring safety risks could be in terms of human life. More checks on old mine workings in the case of Lofthouse brought about new legislation and it was not before time many argued.

Events from the 1984/85 national coal strike are illustrated in a number of sections in the book particularly in the one featuring Orgreave. Examining these pictures, they resemble more of a medieval battle field rather than scenes from a twentieth-century dispute. The way the miners at this period were used as a political football must appear obscene even to the most impartial observer today.

After the dispute the rapid closure of vast numbers of collieries in the so-called dash-for-gas has left large mining communities in Yorkshire struggling to regenerate economically – a struggle which continues to the present day.

Arguably the biggest disappointment in mining terms during the last forty years was the Selby coalfield project. Millions of pounds were literally sunk into the complex at the outset with the prediction that it would yield coal for many years hence. Photographs in the book show various structures being erected only to be seen crashing down some twenty or more years later.

Pictorially, it may be argued that a book featuring collieries could become a little monotonous. That was the reason for gathering a large number from the *Yorkshire Post* archives and selecting ones that would show as much variation on the subject as possible. Although the county has enjoyed a long association with coal, I don't believe there has ever been a period in its long history that has been more eventful than the previous forty to fifty years. I am pleased to be able to document this occurrence which has seen the industry virtually disappear and I hope it is described in an unbiased way. Much of the information has been gleaned from the many bound volumes of *Yorkshire Post* and *Yorkshire Evening Post* newspapers in the *Yorkshire Post*'s vast vaults.

For help and guidance on this book I am, as always, grateful for the help received from Paul Bolton at the *Yorkshire Post* and to David Clay and Keith Hampshire for making available the vast number of hard copy prints as well as images from the digital archive.

It might be that coal is becoming a fading memory to those who lived through the trials and tribulations of the past fifty or more years and the present generations might find it hard to imagine a time when it was relied upon to provide heating, energy and a means of travel. But it cannot be denied that coal has left an indelible mark on Yorkshire's long industrial history.

One

Acton Hall to Drax Power Station

Ackton Hall, Wakefield

During April 1968 hundreds of tons of sludge fell down the Haigh Moor shaft at Ackton Hall colliery, trapping four men in a pit-bottom office. Three of them – William Fawley, Gordon Good and Dennis Farley – were rescued by men who went down the neighbouring Silkstone shaft and made their way through via a connecting passage. Unfortunately, the fourth man, J. Westerman, did not survive the incident. An NCB official said that the debris came from an old mine shaft which had been filled in some three years earlier. The picture shows Mrs Fawley crying with joy on learning her husband was safe.

On 28 July 1893 the owner of Acton Hall colliery, Lord Masham, announced that wages were to be cut by 25 per cent. Miners refused to accept that, and were locked out. Later miners learned that casual labour was being used and protested. Troops were then called in, the Riot Act was read and they opened fire. James Duggan and James Gibbs were killed, and dozens were left lying in the streets badly injured – men, women, and children. In 1993, Featherstone raised £10,000 for a memorial in the town centre and yards from the former Ackton Hall pit gates. Blacksmith Dave Poskitt, pictured, put the sculpture together. It was designed by northern artist, Julia Barton. Ackton Hall colliery closed in 1985.

Allerton Bywater, Leeds

Huge stocks of large size coal are seen stacked high along the roadside at Allerton Bywater in December 1958. Over the previous few months, there had been little demand from the public for domestic coal and stocks of good quality large coal were mounting up at the pitheads. An official at Allerton Bywater colliery told the *Yorkshire Post* on 12 December 1958 that, as a result of supply outstripping demand, stocks were at their highest since the nationalisation of the mines. However, the colder weather was expected to even stocks out. Although Allerton Bywater pit was sunk in 1875 there are records of mining around the village from the 1600s. Surface mining existed as far back as Roman times.

On 21 August 1984 a line of police contains pickets in a side street opposite Allerton Bywater colliery. A legal advice worker was amongst those monitoring policing at the colliery and he said, 'It seems to me that the police action was likely to cause injury and was unnecessary in the circumstances.' A spokesman for West Yorkshire Police said officers at Allerton Bywater had been involved in similar operations throughout the strike and their judgement would be relied upon for tactics and numbers used to contain pickets.

On the same day as the above picture a policeman and picket narrowly escaped being run over by a van – travelling at speed – carrying three strikebreaking miners home. The *Yorkshire Post* of 22 August 1984 stated, 'At Allerton Bywater an estimated 1,500 pickets gathered outside the colliery gates to stop the three miners but were unsuccessful. When the three had finished their shift they got in a van. As it left the pit yard pickets pushed the police across the entrance.' The newspaper also alleged that seven policemen were injured and twelve pickets arrested.

'The British Coal flag was lowered to half mast as the last pit in Leeds closed today,' announced the *Yorkshire Evening Post* 27 March 1992. The flag was hoisted only a few weeks earlier when miners at Allerton Bywater broke their production record. A pithead spokesman said, 'No one would have known about the record if we hadn't put the flag up. Now it seems appropriate to take it down. The men don't see any reason for closing the mine.' The colliery opened around 1875. Three years later the mine commenced coal production from the Haigh Moor and Silkstone seams. Five miners were killed in an underground explosion at Allerton on 10 March 1930. The last man killed at the pit was Malcolm King, who died in a roof fall on 14 June 1991, less than a year before the pit's closure. He was thirty-one, and father to two small children.

In the days leading up to Allerton Bywater's closure, the *Yorkshire Evening Post* of 26 April 1991 ran the headline, 'Grim Choices Facing Pitmen' and featured several miners talking about their future prospects. Three of them are pictured here, from left, Tom Siddall, Clive Cowell and Bob Stokes, who at thirty-two had spent half his life down the pit. He followed his father at Allerton. He was a face-worker and was leaving the industry. 'I'm fed up with mining. Fed up with British Coal, they way they have treated us since 1985. It's confrontation rather than conciliation,' he said.

On 10 March 1992 the *Yorkshire Evening Post* reported that more than 550 miners from the doomed Allerton Bywater pit were to converge on Leeds on Friday (13 March) when the city was to hold a tribute evening to those who had devoted their lives to the industry. A fleet of seven double-decker buses plus several coaches were to carry the miners from Castleford bus station to Leeds Town Hall where Council chiefs planned a £5,000 gala evening to mark the end of deep coal mining in Leeds. 'And the NUM from Allerton will have their own precious gift to bestow on Leeds – their elaborate lodge banner. At about 8 pm the NUM committee will raise the 6-ft by 9-ft banner which denotes more than 100 years of the NUM at Allerton and will march with it for the last time before presenting it to council leader, John Tricket,' said the newspaper.

A miner clocks off for the last time at Allerton Bywater colliery on 27 March 1992. The colliery closed with the loss of 1,060 jobs. In its final year of production the colliery cleared a profit of £9.9 million. Millions of tonnes of coal were abandoned.

Askern, Doncaster

Miners returned to work after a month-long strike on Monday 11 March 1974. Happy to be back was Claude Carr, pictured on the right as he came off the day shift at Askern. Claude, one of the charge hands in the colliery's Warren House seam, said, 'Things aren't too bad. We managed about 75 per cent of our average Monday production.' Askern normally produced 16,000 tons of coal a week and Claude expected the colliery to be achieving full production by the end of the week. Earlier in the day, a broadcast bombardment of 'take care' reminders began as miners queued for canteen coffee and continued as they queued for lamps and made their way to the shaft. The main picture shows other miners on their first day back at Askern.

This picture headed an article from 16 January 1984, titled 'A cloud over Askern pit', where it was mentioned that plans were being prepared to develop the colliery's Barnsley seam in the Pollington area. The multi-million-pound scheme, however, was dependent on the pit getting back into profit, a situation which was dependent on both the men and the management. Manager David Clibbery said that the future of Askern was in the north of the pit, where the Warren House and Barnsley seams merged. The faces to be developed there would be considerably nearer the pit bottom and the quality of coal would be better than that mined at the time.

Gordon Cuffling, fifty-one, was paying the price on 22 August 1984 for working on the previous day during the miners' strike. He said, 'I had no trouble getting into work but all hell was let loose shortly after. Windows were smashed at the pit and pickets were stoning the police. I realised there was a danger of someone being killed or seriously injured so, after four hours at work, I returned home. I was shocked to discover the damage to my house. Thankfully my wife was out at the time. I want to work, but I won't be going back because my home and family are now at risk. I have a licensed shotgun and am prepared to use it to protect my home.'

Austhorpe, Leeds

Protestors against a proposed open-cast mine in Austhorpe are seen making their way along Barrowby Lane in January 1993. Mrs Judith Mitchell, chairperson of Austhorpe and Cotton Residents' Environmental Society, said, 'We are fighting tooth and nail to preserve the green belt around Austhorpe. We are asking for a review of MPG3 the infamous planning regulation which is biased in favour of open-cast contractors. The basis for closing down the deep-mine industry seems to be that there is no market for coal. So why allow open-cast mining in green belt and residential areas?'

Barley Hall, Rotherham

Miners at Barley Hall (Thorncliffe), north of the village of Thorpe Hesley, are pictured on their last shift, 31 May 1974. The pit was sunk 1886/87. In 1977, a two-part BBC 'Play for Today' television production, *The Price of Coal*, was filmed at the closed colliery. The 1976 Disney film *The Littlest Horse Thieves*, or its UK title *Escape from the Dark*, had a considerable amount of location filming done there with many of the villagers being used as extras and some of the film crew living in the village during production.

Barnsley Main, Barnsley

An early picture of a group of deputies at the colliery where the first shaft was sunk in 1838 by the Barnsley Main Colliery Co. Ltd. The colliery was originally axed in May 1966 under Lord Robens' streamlining plan. The colliery's Barnsley seams were taken over by the nearby Barrow colliery and approximately 450 miners were transferred. But it was reopened in 1985 as part of the Barnsley coalfield reconstruction – at a cost of £25 million. Final closure came in July 1991 and a headgear, heapstead and winding engine house have been preserved on part of the site.

Barrow, Barnsley

In March 1962 modern high-speed output resulting from 100 per cent mechanisation earned Barrow its unofficial title 'show pit of the north'. In the previous year a million tons of coal was brought up the shaft and it was literally untouched by hand from the moment it was mined to the time it was mechanically shovelled into industrial furnaces. Shotfiring was cut to a minimum and the Anderson Shearer loader, which chewed away coal in 2-ft 3-in bites, reduced the risk of pneumoconiosis by causing only one sixth of the dust created by the pick and shovel method of mining. The picture shows manager Colin Shepherd with some of his men.

Bentley, Doncaster

In November 1997, Mayor of Doncaster Cllr Sheila Mitchinson (right) and Mayoress Audrey Gregory were amongst those who made their pilgrimage to the Bentley colliery disaster memorial at Arksey cemetery. They all said prayers and sang hymns at the annual commemoration service to honour the forty-five men killed in an explosion at Bentley on 20 November 1931, and the seven men who died when a paddy train crashed on 21 November 1978. Also remembered were other miners killed in pit accidents.

Looking at plans for the first phase of the £6 million redevelopment of the Bentley colliery site in June 1998, are (left to right) Dianne Williams, Bentley Central councillor, Ian Bramley, English Partnerships senior development executive, and chief engineer for IMC (International Mining Construction) Graham Agnew. The first phase of the project was a £1.3 million land reclamation by English Partnerships, aimed to provide a 25-acre recreation and leisure area and pave the way for new homes. The pithead buildings had already been demolished.

Brookhouse, Rotherham

Their faces black with coal dust, the miners pictured here emerged into the bright sunlight on Friday 25 October leaving the last ever coal-producing shaft at Brookhouse. Whilst 300 of the colliery's 500 miners had asked to be transferred to other pits, most of those on the last coaling shift seemed to have opted for redundancy. Bitter and sad, some stopped to talk to reporters. Fitter Dave Pearson said, 'It was a happy pit …We had just got to know all those from Orgreave who came here when it was shut and now we've all got to move.'

The picture was taken in October 2004 at the Beighton Time Works sculpture, where a memorial to Brookhouse colliery 'overwind' accident was unveiled. Seen here are former miners at the pit, Frank Turner and Bill Rose. (Photograph by Glenn Ashley)

Caphouse, Wakefield

'A £2m scheme to create the country's finest mining museum was launched in Yorkshire yesterday,' said the *Yorkshire Post* of 6 December 1985. Production at Caphouse colliery stopped a few weeks earlier and the Yorkshire Mining Museum Trust was planning to turn the pit into a working museum. The project was a joint effort run by South and West Yorkshire County Councils, Wakefield and Kirklees District Councils and the NCB. The trust chairman John Gunnell said, 'No area of this country has made a greater contribution to the history of mining and the energy wealth of this nation than South and West Yorkshire. It is therefore fitting that Yorkshire should have an exciting and imaginative project to recognise that contribution and that history.' The top picture shows Cllr Gunnell unveiling a plaque at Caphouse, watched by, from left, Cllr Jim Marston; John Stanbury, chief executive Wakefield District Council, and Peter Hall, deputy area director of the NCB. The general view of Caphouse dates from 14 Jan 1987.

Right: Miners at the Caphouse – Denby Grange colliery (merged in 1981) celebrated with champagne in July 1985 after smashing a British record for producing coal. They produced 13.09 tonnes a man on every shift over a five-day period.

Below: Mine guide Col Reed is pictured welcoming pit ponies Eric and Ernie to Caphouse colliery in July 2007. Earlier in the year, veteran Sparky, thought to be the oldest deep-mine pit pony in Britain, died at the museum aged thirty-six and staff decided that the time had come to look for some more ponies. The museum took on Eric and Ernie, named after comedians Morecambe and Wise, on probationary adoption from the RSPCA, which rescued them from a coalfield area in Wales where they had been abandoned.

The Alamo at Cortonwood Colliery

Cortonwood, Barnsley

In March 1984, the NCB announced that Cortonwood, sunk in 1873, was due to close; this becoming the 'final straw' which brought about the long-running UK miners' strike (1984/85). Cortonwood pickets are pictured at the colliery on 21 March 1984.

Women against pit closures striding past Cortonwood with banners flying on 5 March 1985.

Miners on the last shift at Cortonwood, 25 October 1985. Earlier in the month the workforce had voted to abandon the struggle against the pit's closure by a three to one majority. The major factor in the decision to abandon the fight had been financial, with the greatest pressure bearing on the men who wanted to opt for voluntary redundancy, take their pay and try to build a future in other industries. The Cortonwood NUM branch secretary said that men in that position had been told they could lose thousands of pounds if they were not put on notice immediately. The Cortonwood site has since been converted into a shopping and leisure area.

Darfield, Barnsley

Five men were treated at Barnsley General Hospital after an explosion on 13 June 1980 at Darfield Main. The accident happened as contractors were drilling bores for explosive charges in a part of the mine which was under development. The men were 225 yards underground and 320 yards from the pit bottom when the explosion happened. All the injured men were employees of Cementation Mining Ltd, Bentley, Doncaster. Two men were discharged from the hospital but three were detained, including Geoffrey Buch of South Elmsall, pictured, who mainly suffered shock. At that time Darfield was part of a four-pit complex which took in Grimethorpe, Houghton Main and Barrow.

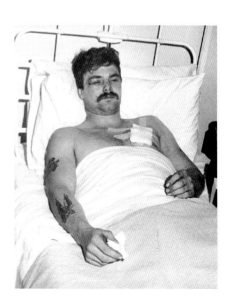

This picture dates from 16 May 1985 when a bombshell was dropped on Darfield miners; their colliery was pinpointed for closure. They had previously held the belief that Darfield – an integral part of the larger Barnsley area coal mining complex – was safe for at least another thirty years. The NCB argued that the scaled-down plan for Barnsley had been brought about by a 'new realism', that coal markets had changed and selling coal was harder, it said. Darfield NUM spokesman, Steven Reeves said, 'We have a glorious leader who knew what he was talking about [in 1984] when he said all pits were at risk.' In November 1986 Darfield was merged with Houghton Main, and finally closed in July 1989.

Denby Grange, Wakefield

In May 1979 it was announced that work was underway on a £7 million scheme to exploit new coal that would save two Barnsley pits – Denby Grange and Caphouse – from closure. The new coal reserves were in an area where seams worked by both pits came together, giving a face section of about 2 metres. Both pits were served by one NUM branch and secretary Granville Wilkinson said, 'This development can't come soon enough for us.' Manager of both pits, Joe Dezelak, said, 'These new workings should give us a productivity level of more than four tonnes a man, which will make this a very profitable unit.'

On 21 January 1985 the *Yorkshire Evening Post* reported that back-to-work miners were producing coal for the first time at Denby Grange colliery, the scene in October the previous year of some of Yorkshire's worst picket-line violence. The pit, where 250 miners were being supported by thirty deputies, was allegedly the first in the Yorkshire Coalfield's Barnsley area to get back into production since the coal strike began. 'So many men have gone back at Denby Grange that the pit is now operating three shifts a day and is expected to produce 5,000 tons of coal this week,' said the *Yorkshire Evening Post*.

In an article headed 'Miners Last March Out', the *Yorkshire Evening Post* of 19 July 1991 said that Denby Grange Colliery 'reached the final chapter in its history today'. The closure of the pit, which had been producing approximately one million tonnes of coal a year, meant the loss of around 450 jobs in an area already crippled by 20,000 mining and engineering job losses since 1979. The alleged reasons for closure, decided the previous summer, were adverse geological conditions and a thick dirt band.

Dodworth, Barnsley

A landmark went up in a cloud of smoke in January 1986 as a 100-ft-high boiler house chimney at Dodworth was demolished. And it took colliery manager Stuart Sumnall's daughters, Rachel and Joanna, only a slight push on a button to reduce the towering landmark to a pile of rubble. The two sisters are pictured in the above picture with explosives expert Brian Hill. The destruction of the chimney was the first stage in the demolition of the pit. The land occupying much of the former pit site now forms the Dodworth Business Park.

Doncaster

A march in Doncaster against pit closures that included MP Dennis Skinner and NUPE general
secretary Rodney Bickerstaff, 27 February 1993.

Drax Power Station, Selby

A National Power coal train pulls up at the Drax Power Station with its load of coal from the Stillingfleet mine near Selby in November 1997. The picture was one of several that illustrated a *Yorkshire Post* article headed 'Six Pits on the Line in spite of RJB Deal'. The article pointed out that the 'dash for gas' and strong pound was seriously threatening the amount of coal supplied to power stations. But it was pointed out, 'Most of the coal supplies to National Power were burnt at Drax, the largest coal-fired power station in Europe and at Eggborough, near Goole.'

In April 1984, at the time of the miners' strike, three members of the flying pickets – Ken Gregson (centre with scarf), Brian Hibbard (back to camera) and Red Stripe (shaven-headed) – chat with picketing miners round their fire outside Drax Power Station. They arrived to express their support and pick up some publicity.

Two

Elsecar Main to Grimethorpe

'3 Elsecar Main Colliery.

Elsecar, Barnsley

Coal extraction proper, under the Earl Fitzwilliam Colleries Co. Ltd, began at the mine between 1905 and 1908 when the shafts were sunk to the Parkgate seam at 333 metres. Other seams worked were the Silkstone, Thorncliffe and the Swallow Wood seam. Ten miners were killed in an explosion on 22 December 1852. During the late 1920s, Elsecar employed approximately 1,900 men including those on the surface and underground.

On 28 October 1983 the end came for Elsecar. Miners who worked the last shift held a nostalgic farewell party at the local Milton Hall. But the colliery had left its mark everywhere. Elsecar village had suffered for years from severe subsidence problems with houses and buildings cracking, leaning and at times falling down. The rundown of the colliery began some years earlier when the workforce was reduced from 800 to the 300 who clocked on for the last time. It was argued by the NCB that working conditions had deteriorated so badly that the colliery was no longer a feasible operation and that sped up the closure timetable. Men at Elsecar are seen on the last working shift.

Emley Moor, Huddersfield

Mining conditions on the Beeston seam at Emley Moor colliery saw little change over generations stretching back almost a century. 'Miners lie on their bellies, sides and backs, the solid rock ceiling grazing their shoulders, as they hack and shovel at a coalface which narrows in places to just 16 ins high,' explained the *Yorkshire Evening Post* on 24 January 1973. It also explained that the Beeston seam produced coal used to make top-grade steel and most of the 2,500-tonne weekly output was exported to Scandanavia for that purpose, commanding a price far in excess of any other Yorkshire coal. The picture shows Reuben Kenworthy at work on the seam with pit deputy Michael Turner (right). In subsequent months other seams were developed using modern mechanical methods of mining. The colliery closed in 1985.

Right:

Featherstone, Wakefield

A coalman delivering in Featherstone went alongside a *Yorkshire Post* article of 18 March 1993 which discussed the implications of the extension of VAT on domestic fuel. Shadow Minister for Environmental Protection Chris Smith mocked the move as a 'so called green measure' because on the government's own figures it would reduce total UK emissions of carbon dioxide by less than 1 per cent.

Below:

Ferrybridge, Knottingley

A coal barge delivers the 35 millionth tonne of coal to Powergen's Ferrybridge power station from RJB Mining's Kellingley colliery.

Flockton Six Lane Ends, Huddersfield

The childhood ambition of Arthur Manby was a little different from that of other children. He wanted his own mine. He realised this ambition around 1969, when he had the chance to buy his own mine. The *Yorkshire Post* of 3 April 1971 reported that he was the owner of the profitable but small Six Lane Ends colliery in Flockton, near Huddersfield. He employed eleven face workers and produced between 7,000 and 10,000 tons of top-grade coal every year. The colliery was one of three privately owned mines in Yorkshire, which operated on a five-year licence granted by the NCB. Father and son Arthur and Steven Manby are pictured at work on the coalface in their mine.

Frickley and South Elmsall, Wakefield

Frickley & South Elmsall colliery was opened by the Carlton Main Colliery Company Ltd. The first sod was cut on 23 April 1903 of No.1 and No.2 shafts and the Barnsley Bed was hit on 23 May 1905 at a depth of 606 metres. South Elmsall colliery, situated in the same curtilage as Frickley, was sunk during 1920–23, reaching the Shafton seam at a depth of 218 metres. Despite being located in South Elmsall, the colliery was sunk within the land of Frickley Hall, part of the small Hamlet of Frickley, hence the Frickley name. In 1925 production ceased in the Shafton seam.

The Barnsley seam was worked until 1934 by hand-got tub stalls when mechanical conveying was introduced at the coalface. During the next three years the installation of face conveyors was completed almost throughout the whole pit. In 1968 there were a number of significant changes including: a rapid loading bunker for merry go round trains – one of the first in the country; a new main fan installed and Frickley and South Elmsall collieries merged under one manager. D. Marklew is pictured on 6 June 1962 with a loco pulling a string of mine-cars in the Carlton area of the pit.

In July 1987, 900 miners at Frickley colliery voted to defy the Yorkshire Area Executive and continue their strike in support of five men suspended for allegedly leaving work early on the eve of the pit's annual holiday. The suspension had led to a further 13,000 miners across South Yorkshire coming out in support of the Frickley strikers. Frickley NUM secretary Steve Tulley is seen talking to the media after a meeting with the NUM's Yorkshire Area President Jack Taylor.

December 1989 saw Frickley men join one of mining's most exclusive clubs by becoming the first at a Yorkshire colliery to cut a mile of coal in a single shift. The jubilant faces of the following Frickley men are seen here, from left to right: John Donelan, Melvyn Hopkins, Barry Jordan, David Taylor, Peter Radford, Paul Zywicki.

On Friday 29 November 1993 the *Yorkshire Evening Post* carried the headline 'Goodbye to all that as Frickley closes'. It reported that sadness, resignation and relief were some of the emotions as miners at one of West Yorkshire's last three pits clocked off for the last time. The majority of the 700 men at Frickley voted to accept enhanced pay offs from British Coal which had accelerated the closure of the pit. The newspaper said that the closure was expected to have a devastating effect on South Elmsall's long-term economy. Kevin Jones, sixteen years a coalface worker, said it was one of the 'saddest days of my life.' But chockfitter Andy Clegg, fourteen years at Frickley, said, 'It's been horrible working here these last few years, the way we have been treated I just can't wait to get away from this damned hole.' Pictured in June 1994, Frank Fish of South Kirkby poses with a placard while lamenting the closure of the pit.

A *Yorkshire Evening Post* article headed 'From black...to green for pit site', during early September 2009, announced that around £7 million was being spent transforming the former Frickley pit site into parkland with 70,000 trees, bridleways, footpaths and cycle routes. Funded by the National Coalfields Programme the regeneration scheme was developed and managed by Yorkshire forward and Wakefield Council and had taken two and a half years to complete. Former Frickley colliery miners Barry Wilshaw (thirty-five years down the pit) and John 'Chick' Pickin (thirty-eight years down the pit) are pictured on the site.

Fryston, Castleford

A happy Jim Bullock, pictured in April 1975 as he returned to Fryston colliery, near Castleford, twenty-one years after he left as manager. With him are his wife Jay and daughter Josephine (seventeen). After a journey 560 yards below ground Jim was convinced that mining was the life for him. During his time at the colliery, he rose from an eighteen-year-old pit lad looking after ponies for five shillings and eight pence a week, to manager.

Fryston colliery miners are pictured enjoying the sunshine during a miners' gala parade through Wakefield on 16 June 1984. The *Yorkshire Post* of 18 June said that the city centre was brought to a standstill as between 40,000 and 50,000 miners, their families and supporters marched in the sun from the Town Hall to Thornes Park. The procession was led by the city's mayor, Cllr Mrs Joyce Beech, and union officials. It took three hours for the procession, one of the biggest seen in Wakefield, to reach the park.

Gascoigne Wood, Selby

A caption beneath this picture in the *Yorkshire Post* of 7 April 1983 read, 'Coal-cutting equipment dwarfs chauffeur, Mr Maurice Hart at Gascoigne Wood, in the Selby coalfield ... when the NCB unveiled the equipment to be installed on the first production face.' It was explained that contractors had already assembled the £3.5 million 138-yard-long wall of armoured props, microchip controls and giant shearer at Gascoigne Wood, inside the world's largest coal shed – as big as King's Cross station – to ensure that the equipment worked and to enable training to start. 'It will be dismantled and transferred piece by piece through the 5,000 yard long underground drift that links Gascoigne Wood and Wistow,' added the *Yorkshire Post*. The Duchess of Kent opened the Selby Coalfield in October 1976. The complex included the following mines: Gascoigne Wood, North Selby, Ricall, Stillingfleet, Whitemoor, Wistow.

This picture appeared in a *Yorkshire Post* supplement of 24 September 1982, headed 'Coal Mining, the 1982 Review'. A caption stated that the sloping structure on the right covered the entrance at Gascoigne Wood – starting point of a 15-mile underground 'drivage' which bisected the coalfield. When the picture was taken, work was already advanced, in the large buildings at the mouth of the tunnel, installing the 12,000 hp conveyor drive motors. On the left, straddling the railway sidings was the first of the outloading bunkers which would, at full production load a 1,000-tonne coal train every half hour.

During August 1984, pickets trying to block a road at Gascoigne Wood come up against an army of police.

Left: The NCB's chief engineer in the North Yorkshire area, John Dunn, left, switched on the conveyor of the surface drift mine cable belt at Gascoigne Wood on 12 August 1985. With him at the official opening was Ian Thompson, the managing director of its manufacturer, Cable Ltd, of Camberley, Surrey. The belt – 5,500 metres long – was to be extended to 14,000 metres and would carry coal from the five mines in the coalfield to a rail line at Gascoigne Wood for distribution to local power stations. It was the biggest order to be received in the UK by Cable Belt Ltd and the full contract was worth £15 million. Coal could be carried at 20 miles an hour on the belt, driven by an 8,750 kw power unit.

Below: These men are drinking a toast to three tunnelling records they broke early in 1986. Carving out a 20-ft-diameter circular roadway at Gascoigne Wood they tunnelled 19 metres in a shift, 43 metres in a day and 152.4 metres in a week to shatter records which had stood since March 1981. The three teams of nineteen men were all employed by Barnsley-based contractors Amco. Colliery manager, Tom Pearson, said, 'The men have done exceptionally well.' The teams used a £3-million full-face tunnelling machine to create their world records.

The champagne corks popped in the Selby coalfield on 1 July 1987 as miners reached the end of the Gascoigne Wood tunnel – then Europe's longest mining tunnel. Members of the tunnelling team – from left, Nigel Cheney, Derek Charlesworth, Derek Sampson, Larry English, Barry Conway, David Walker and Andrew Mortimer – toast the completion of the tunnel with the deputy manager of the Gascoigne Wood drift mine, Alan Spratt, and the project manager, Istvan Czirok.

Glasshoughton, Castleford

Some of the following pictures covered an entire page in the *Yorkshire Post* of 18 April 1938. On a previous page was a long article titled 'The Barnsley Coal Trade'. The article stated there was a movement of trade eastward to the new Doncaster field but this was not an indication that Barnsley was declining from its position as the coal metropolis. 'The trend Doncaster-wards was a search for readier access to the rich Barnsley bed which had been worked to the point of exhaustion, but there remained within a five mile radius of Barnsley other seams sufficient to maintain the present output for another century at least,' argued the *Yorkshire Post*. The picture shows miners manoeuvring tubs at Glasshoughton.

In 1938 the *Yorkshire Post* informed that the exhaustion of the thick coal seam in the old Barnsley coalfield had given an impetus to mechanisation and a real change which had taken place was not the drift of mining activity from one place to another, but a revolution in the method of working. Virtually all the collieries in the western area around Sheffield had been mechanised. 'The arduous method of hewing coal with the pick has been replaced by the coal-cutter, driven by compressed air or electricity; the pony and hand trammer have made way for mechanised conveyors and haulages. The collier's occupation has undergone a definite change,' said the *Yorkshire Post*. A miner is seen here manoeuvring tubs at Glasshoughton February 1938.

By 1938, increasing mechanisation meant less relative employment in the coal industry. There were hundreds of men in the Yorkshire coalfield, calculated, as unemployed mineworkers, who by reason of age and unsuitability could not be employed under new conditions of working. It was estimated that the change had reduced the number of men required by 16 per cent. But, in turn, mechanisation made increasing demands on the engineering trade. Therefore, on balance, mechanisation had probably created as much employment as unemployment. The photograph shows miners at Glasshoughton, February 1938.

At one time the valuable Barnsley area coal formed the basis of the exports to Northern Europe, but first the occupation of the Ruhr and then the contraction of continental markets in the uneasy interwar years checked the development of new collieries and, incidentally but vitally, threw most of the output on the home market. 'This intensification of inland competition lowered prices to an uneconomical level and brought about a chaotic situation from which the only escape was by way of central control of prices and marketing. This was at first voluntarily accepted by the owners and has now Parliamentary sanction and force. The result is general stabilisation of conditions,' reported the *Yorkshire Post*. Glasshoughton men are seen preparing coal for the market during February 1938.

Miners taking their working clothes from their lockers at the pithead baths before changing to go down the pit, February 1938.

Vehicles being loaded at the quick-loading hoppers at the pithead, February 1938.

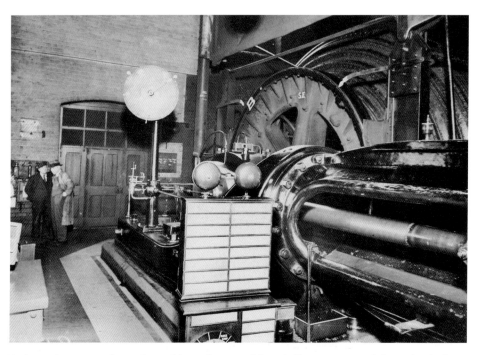

In the engine room – the engine and huge drum used for winding cages up and down the shaft.

The 1938 *Yorkshire Post* article made the point that the most striking feature of the coalfield at that time was its coking industry. Many groups of collieries had their large, modern, completely mechanised by-products plants. Their chief output was coke for blast furnaces, 'but there is a valuable residue of by-products such as tar, oils sulphate of ammonia and bezole ... It is also getting money now from something it formerly wasted – coke oven gas,' said the newspaper. This view shows the by-products plant of the Glasshoughton and Castleford Collieries Ltd, February 1938.

This picture was taken to accompany a story of a dispute at Glasshoughton in April 1964. William O'Brien, thirty-five, branch secretary of the NUM there, said that between 500 and 600 men were on strike and nearly 3,000 in the Castleford area. The root cause of the dispute was the switching of contract workers to day wage jobs with consequent drops in pay of between £2 and £3 a day. Men at Fryston, Wheldale, Whitwood, Allerton Bywater, Prince of Wales and Ledston Luck came out in support.

Above: On 28 March 1986, colliery workers deputy Brian Toole (left) and face worker Dave Donohue are pictured on the last day at Glasshoughton. Brian, forty-eight, who started working there as a pit-bottom boy thirty-three years earlier, said, 'Of course it's a sad day, but it's just one of those things.' On the last day there were approximately 300 men on the books. After the Easter break, a handful were to return in a salvage operation expected to last until late autumn. To face worker Roy Blackburn the closure matter was very simple. He said, 'It shouldn't be shutting at all, it's ridiculous.' The *Yorkshire Evening Post* said the men voted in favour of the pit closure at a mass meeting in Castleford's Trades & Labour Club two years earlier, just a few weeks before the big strike.'

Left: The demolition of No. 1 shaft pithead gear and engine house on 1 July 1980.

Gomersal Colliery or Nutter Lane Pit, Cleckheaton

Under the header 'Miners "sold out" over new jobs' the *Yorkshire Post* of 20 July 1973 said that more than 100 miners at Gomersal colliery, which had closed at the end of the previous month, had accused the NCB of going back on their word over the question of new jobs. The men who were engaged in recovering equipment from the pit went on strike but agreed to resume duties pending further talks. The men were assured they would get an interview and a choice of a new job but subsequently heard they were to receive a letter telling them to which pit they would be sent. 'The men resent this take-it-or-leave-it attitude. The board has gone back on everything they promised,' said a spokesman. A few of the miners who staged a lightning strike are shown here with a list of names of men offered jobs at other pits. By 1979 a reclamation scheme arranged by Kirklees Council was completed. This landscaped the entire area and erased almost all trace of the mine, as though it had never existed.

Grimethorpe, Barnsley

Pickets try to stop a lorry driver from entering Grimethorpe coalite plant, 11 January 1972.

Grimethorpe colliers are pictured with Yorkshire Coal Queen Gillian Parkin, twenty, after the millionth tonne of coal was hauled out of the pit on 12 March 1980, two weeks before the end of the financial year. Gillian handed out cigars and champagne at the pit head. A little later in the day Coal Board officials cancelled a celebration buffet to mark the event when about half a dozen miners from the afternoon shift complained about not being invited. A Coal Board spokesman said, 'We cancelled the meal after hearing the views of the protestors, and the food was distributed to old folk in Grimethorpe.' It was the first time Grimethorpe had produced a million tonnes in a year in its long history.

On 6 November 1980 the design and construction of an internationally financed £20 million pressurised fluidised-bed test facility was completed at Grimethorpe. The project, the most ambitious of its kind in the world, was funded by the USA, Germany and the UK. The facility was designed to explore the potential a new type of coal-burning boiler that promised major advances in conversion efficiency and the additional advantages of being able to burn ash and high-sulphur coals in a way that protected the environment. The picture shows an interior view of the facility on 5 November 1980.

Grimethorpe pickets
gather round a brazier on
24 October 1984.

On 23 October 1992 news came that Grimethorpe and Houghton Main were to cease production during the following week. This was despite government reassurances that all pits scheduled for closure would undergo a ninety-day review. Ken Hancock, NUM branch secretary at Grimethorpe, said, 'We are shell-shocked and very angry.' A spokesman for British Coal confirmed production at Barnsley's two remaining pits would cease on 30 October. Grimethorpe miners are seen in the lamp room after their last shift.

Grimethorpe colliery band was formed in 1917, as a leisure activity for the workmen at the colliery. From 1932 to 1945 the band entered forty-two such competitions, winning nineteen and never finishing lower than fifth! A turning point in the band's history came in 1972 with the appointment of Elgar Howarth as professional conductor and music adviser. Following the closure of Grimethorpe colliery, financial backing continued from British Coal until 1995 when Richard Budge, Chief Executive of RJB Mining PLC agreed to fund the band, an agreement which continued until 2011. Greater international fame came to the band with the making of the 1995 film *Brassed Off!* The film told the story of the fictional South Yorkshire village of Grimley, and how the local colliery's band won a national competition only a few days after the closure of the colliery was announced. The best bonus from *Brassed Off* has been a number of tours: Japan and Australia, New Zealand & Hong Kong. The band has also recently become the first-ever brass band to become an ensemble-in-residence at the Royal College of Music in London. With the continued support of RJB mining, and the success of *Brassed Off!*, the band was in good health and the future secured. The photo is taken outside the colliery manager's office after the band won the British Open in September 1991.

Three

Handsworth to Lofthouse

Handsworth, Sheffield

Tommy Walker, local NUM branch secretary, wishes luck to some of the members of Handsworth's afternoon shift before they went down for the last time on Friday 27 October 1967. Of the 300 men still working there, most were transferring to other collieries in the area – Orgreave and Treeton. The remaining fifty to sixty stayed at Handsworth for a time on salvage work. There were to be no dismissals. The pit only had one strike in the previous 25 years. Tom Walker, Handsworth NUM secretary said, 'The secret of our success here has been co-operation among the management, under officials and workmen. In its closing weeks, working the lone face left in the wet, difficult conditions of Handsworth, productivity had averaged 46.6 cwt a man-shift overall – about 7 cwt above the then Yorkshire coalfield average. 'They have worked well to the end,' said Raymond Wilkins, aged forty-five, the colliery manager for the previous three years. There was nothing to mark the closure day. 'We wanted to go out nice and quietly,' Ray added. The closure, first announced in March, came because the pit's reserves had run out.

Handsworth was the last working pit in Sheffield's city boundaries. Coal mined within Sheffield had, for the previous 200 years at least, accompanied the city's rise in prosperity. But the first records of it being dug date back to the end of the thirteenth century, when Sir Thomas Chaworth granted the monks of Beauchief Abbey the right to get coal for themselves and their tenants; this they did around the abbey. Handsworth colliery is seen here on 22 June 1967.

Hatfield, Doncaster

Kevin Hughes (second from left) was born in Doncaster, the son of a miner. He was educated at Owston Park secondary modern, and took up his father's profession in 1970. He was an official for the NUM and also attended the University of Sheffield for three years under a day-release scheme. He was the Member of Parliament (MP) for Doncaster North from 1992 to 2005. He served as a government whip, in opposition and government, from 1996 until 2001 and campaigned on pit safety issues before the privatisation of British Coal in the early 1990s. He is pictured chatting to Hatfield miners on 13 August 2001 at a time when he and others were fighting to reopen the colliery. He died in July 2006.

50

Above: Hatfield procurement manager Jamie Wilson pictured on 19 April 2007 with an AMB25, which was to be installed underground later in the year for cutting new seams. The equipment was shown to Doncaster North MP Ed Milliband when he visited the colliery. As well as the cutting equipment, he was shown work going on underground at the mine, accompanied by Richard Budge, boss of pit owners Powerfuels.

Right:

Hickleton/Goldthorpe, Barnsley

Mayor of Barnsley Cllr Ken Young, who spent thirty-eight years in the mines, and father Allan Hounsone dedicated a memorial – a winding wheel set in a stone plinth – to Hickleton pit. In 1986 it merged with Goldthorpe and production on the site finally ceased in 1988. The site was subsequently redeveloped to form part of the Thurnscoe Business Park.

'Another of South Yorkshire's industrial landmarks disappears as workmen bring down the No. 2 winding gear at Hickleton,' said the *Yorkshire Post* of 7 July 1994. Contractors working for British Coal had left just one winding wheel at the pit. It was to remain there to provide a backdrop for a community-based Dearne Valley Opera production there from 21–23 July.

High Hazels, Rotherham

Eyesore buildings in the grounds of High Hazels disappeared with a bang on 21 September 1969. At exactly noon the colliery's old dynamite store was exploded into a pile of rubble by men of the Sheffield-based 106 West Riding Field Squadron Royal Engineers. They also blew up two other brick buildings and a wall as a favour to the National Coal Board.

Houghton Main, Barnsley

Five men lost their lives and one man sustained serious injury as a result of an explosion in the Meltonfield seam workings at Houghton Main colliery at approximately 6.50 p.m. on 12 June 1975. The picture shows women waiting for news 13 June 1975. A priest was at hand and the Salvation Army stepped in to provide tea and food for tired helpers. At the time of the disaster Houghton Main employed a total of 1,361 men; 1,191 underground and 170 on the surface.

Rescue teams worked throughout the night to recover bodies of the dead miners. Amongst them were Irvin Larkin, fifty-five; Richard Bannister, thirty; Arnold Williamson, fifty-nine; Raymond Copper, forty-two; and Leonard Baker, fifty-three. A sixth man was taken to hospital with severe burns and a fractured thigh. Two other men caught in the fringe of the explosion miraculously walked out unscathed. There were some harrowing scenes at the pithead as weeping relatives were told of the seriousness of the situation. The picture shows rescuers taking a miner's body to an ambulance.

Yorkshire Area NUM President Arthur Scargill, with face blackened with coal dust after an inspection underground, gives Energy Secretary Tony Benn details about the disaster at the pithead. Tony Benn expressed sympathy with victims' families, and said, 'It might remind people, as it reminded me, that there is still a very high price in human life to be paid, for the coal we get in this country.'

Scene at the funeral of Irvin Larkin, 18 June 1975. The official report on the disaster stated that the explosion resulted from the ignition of an accumulation of firedamp. Nine days before the explosion a ventilation fan was switched off after two men saw sparks shooting out. Their actions were commended by author of the report J. Carver, because the fan's job was to keep air flowing to an underground dead-end where explosive fire damp was known to accumulate in huge quantities. But from that day on, no definite action was ever taken, and the fan was finally blamed for causing the blast.

Jubilant miners at the combined Houghton Main/Darfield colliery were celebrating the fastest million tonnes of coal ever mined in the coalfield at Barnsley on 10 November 1987. The millionth tonne came out just twenty-nine weeks after the start of British Coal's financial year. The record broke a previous one, set by Grimethorpe in January 1981, by an incredible two months. The record-breaking coal came from four faces at Houghton and two from the Darfield end. The record was achieved because of workforce determination and new equipment – with £4 million being spent at Houghton. Miners are pictured with Miss Barnsley, Wendy Sharman.

On 26 March 1993, children, each carrying a placard bearing the name of a colliery, assembled outside Houghton pit gates; each pit name had CLOSED stamped over it. The rally, organised by Women Against Pit Closures, was arranged to show the huge number of mining communities devastated by pit closures and highlighted the threat to Houghton, Grimethorpe and Markham Main. In a report published by the NUM and NACODS on 26 April 1993 it was stated that Houghton Main had reserves of 20.9 million tonnes and an economic life of fifty-two years. Unfortunately, all this was in vain as Houghton eventually closed at the end of April 1993.

Kellingley, Selby

A view taken in April 1965 of the underground locomotive garage at Kellingley which was in the No. 8 (Castleford) Area of the Yorkshire Division.

In June 1984 around 8,000 miners followed the funeral cortege of Kellingley miner Joe Green, the second of their colleagues to die on the picket lines during the 1984/5 strike. Joe of Knottingley near Pontefract died in an accident with a lorry while picketing Ferrybridge Power Station. Miners from all over the country took part in the procession from Pontefract racecourse to the town's crematorium. They were led by the Kellingley colliery band. Following up were NUM President Arthur Scargill, Jack Taylor and MPs Geoff Lofthouse and Bill O'Brien. Joe's coffin was escorted into the crematorium by a Scots piper, Gordon Queen who played Scots Lament. Family, friends and union officials packed the crematorium and the service was relayed outside by a PA system. Arthur Scargill described Joe as a 'fantastic lad.' He added, 'He had unswerving loyalty to the union and its policies.'

On 5 March 1985 miners were led back to Kellingley by union officials, with banners flying, in a symbolic return. It took forty minutes to complete the walk of several miles from the social club to the pit gates and the men were accompanied by supporters, their wives and children. An almost carnival atmosphere prevailed for much of the march but, as the procession passed the homes of strike-breakers, and a knot of police, there was vicious chanting. As they approached the gates all united behind a chorus of 'Arthur Scargill, we'll support you ever more.'

The House of Commons Select Committee on Energy visited the coalface at Kellingley in February 1986 to learn some 'pit talk'. The committee was about to launch one of its periodical examinations of the coal industry and chairman, Ian Lloyd (Cllr Havant) said, 'We have come to familiarise members of the committee who know little about the coal industry apart from what they have read. Other committee members included Pontefract Labour MP Geoffrey Lofthouse, Dr Michael Clark (Cllr Rochford), James Pawsey (Cllr Regby and Kenilworth) and Peter Rost (Cllr Erewash).

Miners at Kellingley were the coal kings of Europe again after recapturing their crown with an output record of 70,262 tonnes during a week in September 1988. Kellingley's new British and Euro best was almost 2,000 tonnes up on the previous record of 68,362 tonnes set by Wistow in December of the previous year. Colliery manager Roy Cocker said, 'The title is now back where it belongs – at Kellingley. We have been knocking on the door for several weeks, averaging 55 to 60,000 tonnes a week, so it is no flash in the pan.'

In January 1998, Peter Mandelson visited Kellingley at the request of Pontefract MP Yvette Cooper, one of the Labour MPs fighting to save pits, to see for himself what the industry was all about. Afterwards he said, 'I saw great men working with great technology ... I had a warm welcome and it is a privilege to see such a committed workforce.' He also went to the other side of South Kirkby to see a disused pit, where thousands once worked. Peter Mandleson, is pictured emerging from a trip down Kellingley with Jon Trickett, MP for Hemsworth, and John Grogan, MP for Selby.

On 30 September 2010 sculptor Graham Ibbeson is pictured with his work – a memorial for miners who lost their lives at Kellingley.

Kinsley Drift, Wakefield

Kinsley Drift was opened on the site of the old Hemsworth colliery on 18 August 1979, with all the razzamatazz of a carnival, by Norman Siddall, the then deputy chairman of the Coal Board. A marquee was pressed into service to accommodate the VIPs present to launch the pit on its way. But the ceremony was taking place against a background of controversy. Former Hemsworth miners transferred to South Kirkby claimed they should have been given first chance of working at the new pit. A spokesman for the Coal Board said that twelve out of fifty miners formerly at Hemsworth, but now at South Kirkby, had been promised jobs, but no decision had been taken on the remainder.

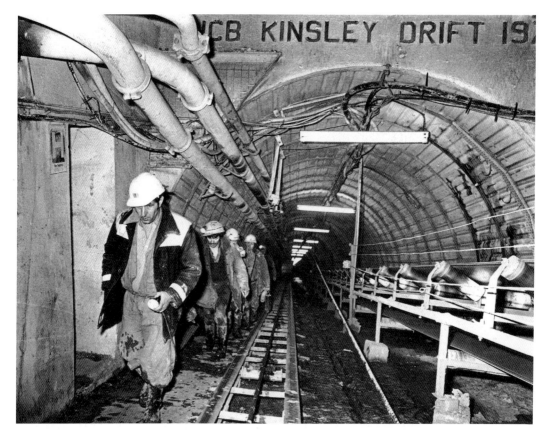

On 10 December 1979 the *Yorkshire Evening Post* reported that two men were killed in an accident at Kinsley Drift mine – Yorkshire's newest super-pit. Five other men were injured – one of them seriously (who later died). The accident happened 600 yards down when two trolley cars taking materials into the drift went out of control. They careered down a steep slope and slammed into a group of men working in the tunnel. A Coal Board spokesman said the trolleys became unhooked from the train and ran down the 1:4 sloping drift. It was the mine's first serious accident since it opened. The picture shows the scene underground at the mine, 10 December 1979.

Louise Gray with Miners at Kinsley Drift mine, 22 February 1982. They were celebrating the mine producing a record-breaking output of 14,200 tonnes from just two coalfaces. Kinsley was also averaging three times the national average for coal produced per man-shift.

According to the NCB in December 1985, Kinsley, opened in 1979 at a cost of £20 million, no longer had a viable future. This was because of its poor quality reserves and difficult working conditions. An NUM spokesman said there ought to be an inquiry into the huge waste of taxpayers' money if the NCB really believed the pit was finished. Hopes for Kinsley's survival were pinned on a coalface which had opened only four weeks earlier in the Sharlston Yard seam, but it had to be abandoned following a series of roof collapses. Retired NUM official Neil O'Connell could not understand why the Board did not 'Open a second face in the Shafton seam; persist with the Sharlston, but in another area, drift deeper to the Beamshaw seam'. The picture illustrates a colliery official inspecting a doomed face at the colliery. The colliery closed in 1986.

Kiveton, Rotherham

Sinking at Kiveton Park began on 6 June 1866. The Barnsley seam was reached on 5 December 1867 at a distance of 405 yards from the surface. The Thorncliffe seam was worked 1886–96. In 1896 another shaft was sunk adjacent to the Barnsley one and connected to it. Kiveton Park amalgamated with Sherwood colliery in 1928. The greatest number of men employed by the colliery was 2,244 in April 1929, the saleable output per man-shift for that year being 21 cwt. The colliery closed on 30 September 1994. The picture above was taken c. 1966.

On 21 December 1967 the last pit ponies in the NCB South Yorkshire area of Kiveton – 'Taffy' who was twenty-five years old and 'Duke' a mere twelve-year-old – are led away from the pithead by the head horse-keeper. Ten years earlier the Sheffield pit had nearly forty ponies. The ponies that had been on salvage work were replaced under a mechanisation programme. An NCB spokesman said, 'Contrary to what many people believe the ponies have been well cared for; they were only allowed to work a certain number of hours.'

In April 1979 miners at Kiveton modelled their new, bright-orange overalls. Left to right, they are: Anthony Barteczko from Killamarsh, Dave Carswell, Stuart Hill and Pat McFall. The NCB's idea was to provide workers throughout the industry with their own personal work gear, which was to be laundered by industrial cleaners each week. The new-style overalls had no loose flaps to get caught up in machinery. There were also equipped with quick-release snap fasteners instead of the conventional buttons or zips.

Ledston Luck, Castleford

The colliery was sunk in the 1870s and later formed part of the interlinked workings around Selby. The two winding houses Nos 1 and 2 seen here were built in 1911 and where among the first to use electric winders, at a time most other mines were still using steam. Both winding houses were listed by English Heritage on 15 September 1987.

During the evening of 27 June 1955, Geoffrey Lloyd, Minister of Fuel and Power, was due to visit Ledston Luck colliery – an outstanding example of the successful reconstruction of an old pit on modern lines. Before going down the pit, Mr Lloyd was to walk amongst the well-kept lawns with crazing paving and flower beds. The pit manager, thirty-one-year-old Geoffrey Barber, believed that if a man worked in pleasant, tidy surroundings he would be tidy with his work – and the miners of Ledston reputedly at that time produced more coal than twice the national average per man-shift. The picture shows the colliery on the day of Mr Lloyd's visit and features the lawns and gardens at the colliery.

Ledston Luck miners emerge after being trapped underground, 31 October 1983.

Above left:

Lofthouse, Wakefield

The *Yorkshire Post* of 22 March 1973 reported that seven miners were still trapped 250 yards underground more than twenty-four hours after water broke through the 3-ft-high face at which they were working at Lofthouse Colliery. One of the nightshift men who had a narrow escape and had to run for his life as the water gushed through was Keith Stone, twenty-six, pictured. 'I have never been so frightened in my life,' he said. 'I thought we were all gonners, but we just kept running and we're the lucky ones.'

Above right: Immediately after the face flooded at 2.30 a.m. on 21 March, rescue teams were working against the clock on the following day. If the trapped men had taken refuge in an air pocket it was estimated they had enough air to last until 6 p.m. that night. One of the rescue teams is pictured here. Six frogmen were also brought in from Cannock, Staffordshire, to help with operations. Meanwhile, water from the flooded face was pumped through thousands of yards of tubing. Members of a rescue team are pictured here.

Opposite below: On 1 November 1983 the *Yorkshire Evening Post* reported that a miners' overtime ban was back on at Ledston Luck after being suspended during an operation to free six face workers trapped by a roof fall. Hundreds of tons of rock, dirt and shale crashed down into a roadway cutting off the men almost 400 ft underground in a 'dead end tunnel' at the colliery. When the alarm was raised, the overtime ban imposed only hours earlier in support of a national pay claim was lifted and all efforts were concentrated on releasing the men. The six rescued miners were, from left, Michael Dargue, Jim Connell, David Kay, Andrew Firth, Terry Fawcett and Richard Hayward. The pit manager Don Jagger, who led about twenty miners in the rescue operation, was the first to reach the trapped men. He said, 'We knew we had to get through to them before any gas built up. We just kept digging although we knew there was the danger of more stuff falling on us at any time. We wanted to get them out before the end of the shift so they could go home and tell their wives what had happened,' he said.

In an attempt to aid the trapped men, a specially trained team of drilling riggers and geologists began boring a small 'lifeline' down to an air pocket. They were drilling just off the main Batley–Wakefield Road at Alverthorpe and were ordered not to smoke because of the dangers of methane gas leaking from old workings that the drill would penetrate. Local women are seen after setting up a trestle table to supply hot drinks and food to the drilling crew on 22 March 1973.

As dawn broke on 22 March, Coal Board surveyors discovered a hole which had appeared in a ploughed field 2½ miles from the pit yard. It was a shaft from a 130-year-old pit believed to have been 100 yards from where the floods burst down below. By 10 a.m. a second hole appeared and a little later a third. The following day an NCB spokesman said disused mine shafts like the three that appeared near Lofthouse were dotted around the country 'like holes in Swiss cheese'. There were certainly many thousands more not recorded on maps and they were the ones which represented the greatest potential dangers to miners. Miners are seen discussing events at the pit with chairman of the NCB, Derek Ezra.

The wife of one of the seven miners trapped at Lofthouse broke down and wept while shaking hands with Prime Minister Ted Heath on 23 March 1973. She was Evelyn Cotton, wife of Charles Cotton, forty-nine. The PM made a thirty-minute visit to the area and asked about conditions down the pit. He then conferred with NCB officials before leaving and commented, 'There is still hope but that of course depends on the conditions down there.'

In time, the rescue attempt to free seven miners failed, though not without the greatest efforts by all those concerned. One body was recovered but it was felt too dangerous to reach the other six. The incident led to the Mines (Precautions Against Inrushes) Regulations 1978 ('PAIR'), requiring 'examination of records held by the Natural Environment Research Council which might be relevant to proposed workings [and] diligent enquiry into other sources of information which may be available, e.g. from geological memoirs, archives, libraries and persons with knowledge of the area and its history.' The picture shows a destroyed underground junction at Lofthouse on 18 April 1973.

'The memorial of the Lofthouse colliery disaster should be a constant reminder of the price that had to be paid for coal,' said the Bishop of Wakefield, Dr Eric Treacy, on 24 November 1974. He was speaking at the dedication service of the memorial on a site off Batley Road, Wakefield, which was directly above where the bodies of the six of the seven men who died in the disaster are believed to be entombed. Relatives and friends of the seven who died, together with representatives of the NCB and pit unions, laid flowers at the foot of the memorial, each side of which, bears the name of one of the dead men.

On 21 September 1973, the *Yorkshire Post* commented that the smiles on the faces of twelve children who were leaving Leeds for a seaside holiday masked the tragedy of the Lofthouse disaster in which their fathers were killed. The children, aged between three months and fourteen years, were staying for a week at Middleton Towers Holiday camp, Morecambe. Jimmy Savile's brother Johnnie is shown with the children at the coach station in The Calls before their departure. Top row (left to right): Janice Brown (11), Jocelyn Brown (14), Anthony Brown (7), Elaine Haigh (10), Eamonn Finnigan (12), Janet Haigh (11). Bottom row: Karyn Brown (9), Tracy Brown (6), Johnnie Savile with Sydney Brown (3 months), Jill Haigh (4), Sally Anne Finnigan (4), Tracy Armitage (6).

Four

Maltby to Royston Drift

Maltby, Rotherham

Twenty-seven men lost their lives at the colliery as a result of an explosion on 28 July 1923. Only one body, that of a man named Reginald Renshaw, was recovered initially despite the efforts of rescue parties. A gob fire had been burning in the mine for some weeks earlier and management decided to close down the pit until the threat had been removed. A number of workers were kept on to deal with the problem and it was reported that progress had been made until the explosion occurred. The following message was received by the Manager of Maltby colliery: '*The King and Queen are very distressed to hear of the disastrous explosion, and are anxious to learn any particulars of the condition of the sufferers.*' Pictured is one of the victims, Harry Norwood, aged thirty, who was a deputy.

News of the disaster brought rescue parties from a number of collieries throughout the region. The rescue was abandoned after twelve hours when all hope of finding any further victims alive was given up. Yet another body was found a few months later. Maltby rescue team is pictured around 1922.

A meeting held shortly after the disaster was attended by the colliery owners, managers and relatives of the deceased and they are seen here.

Right: Maltby million-tonne celebrations, 23 March 1973.

Below: It was alleged that pit strike violence took a sinister twist on 21 September 1984 when pickets were accused of firing air rifles and catapults at hundreds of police at Maltby. The police, many in riot gear, were massed outside the colliery gates keeping pickets at one end of Tickhill Road, where the pit is sited, while the other end was kept open for contract workers. NUM officials claimed that dozens of police on duty were not displaying identification numbers on their uniforms. But the county's chief constable, Peter Wright, said his men were wearing overalls for protective reasons, and the fact that they had no numbers on was an 'oversight.'

Left: Maltby became the first colliery in the world to gain an internationally recognised British Standards seal of approval for the quality of its coal in January 1992. At the handover of the award – won by the pit's coal preparation plant – are, from the left, colliery manager, Malcolm High; Mike Allan, of coal preparation; Ian Hodgkinson, operations manager with Lloyd's Register of Quality Assurance; and Carl Bevan of coal preparation.

Below: Pictured on 7 November 1995 are the Maltby men who won the NCB South Yorkshire area fire-fighting competition. They are left to right (front): Brian Jeffcoates, John Williamson, Mick Frear, Steve Tipper, Jom Robey, Tom Richardson. Back row: fire officers Brian Lowndes and Ray Winston.

Above: During the Maltby colliery centenary celebrations, Maltby Miners Welfare band lead the procession to the 1923 pit disaster memorial at Grange Lane, Maltby, on 1 June 2008.

Right:

Manvers Main, Rotherham

A test track for underground locomotives was laid at Manvers in January 1968, in an attempt to avoid rail accidents at local pits. The quarter-mile single track was used to teach colliery loco men how to handle the engines in difficult conditions. Grease was put on the carefully calculated gradients of the line (pictured) and the locomen were shown how to stop the 15-ton diesel engine in the shortest distance. That was just one aspect of the one-week courses being run for pitmen from three areas of the Yorkshire coalfield. Course instructor, Horace Hartley, a diesel driver with twenty years' experience said, 'After the drivers have had some practice on the track I find that it builds up their confidence and makes them more expert at handling the locomotives.'

Miners at Manvers are pictured on 8 February 1974. The coke ovens and coal by-products plant were closed in 1981. With rationalisation in the South Yorkshire coalfield, from 1950 to 1956, Manvers became the centre of coal output from a number of local collieries (known as the South Manvers complex) linked below ground and including Wath Main and Kilnhurst. The colliery complex was closed on 25 March 1988 and the land remained derelict until the mid-1990s when a regeneration programme with the assistance of the European Social Fund was undertaken.

Six workmen were taken to hospital at Mexborough on 4 June 1963 after a 100-yard section of gantry, weighing hundreds of tons, plunged 80 feet to the ground. It happened during a fire at the huge Manvers coal preparation plant. Damage ran into many thousands. Production was halted and firemen from Mexborough, Wath-on-Dearne and Rotherham fought the blaze. Railway traffic on the main Sheffield–Leeds line, which ran through the plant, had to be diverted. The gantry, supported on big steel girders, was used to convey coal along belts to the coking ovens.

Right: A new highly-equipped coalface, which would never produce a lump of coal, went on show at Manvers Training Centre in September 1986. Instructor, Colin Roper, left, and two apprentice electricians – Paul Clayworth and Darren Axe – right, preview a site where even children would be allowed to look at the modern operation, because they did not need to go underground. The 35-metre face was being used solely for teaching purposes – but was nonetheless fully equipped with up-to-date working machinery. The centre was open to the public for a limited period as part of an Industry Year event.

Below:

Markham Main, Doncaster

Markham Main protest camp with Brenda Nixon, Aggie Currie, Lissy Virago and Anne Scargill, 11 January 1993.

Markham Main was bought by Malcolm Edwards' (former Commercial Director of British Coal) Coal Investments, which owned six pits, in May 1994. Coal Investments went into administration in February 1996 and later the colliery site was redeveloped for housing. Malcolm Edwards is pictured here on 9 June 1994.

Markham Main general manager Jonathan Oxby announces fifty new jobs at the colliery on 12 June 1995.

North Gawber, Barnsley

North Gawber colliery was sunk to the Barnsley seam from 1850–52. The pit was the scene of a terrible disaster on 12 September 1935 when nineteen men were killed following an explosion in the Lidgett Seam. In December 1985 the NUM agreed to some of North Gawber's men being transferred to Woolley, some to other pits and an undisclosed number taking voluntary redundancy. Woolley closed in 1987. Secretary of State for Northern Ireland and MP for Barnsley, Roy Mason, accepts a chew of tobacco from some of North Gawber's miners after a visit underground in May 1978.

The tangle of collapsed conveyor belting, falls of roof and compacted coalface supports, reflected the scene underground at North Gawber after six months of neglect, due to the miners' strike, alleged the *Yorkshire Post* of 24 August 1984. The colliery's problems stretched from the winding gear to the farthest corner of the mine. 'All in all it is a pretty dismal picture for a colliery that had fought its way from large losses into a profit before the strike began,' said pit manager Frank Flynn. But he had written to each of his 750 miners and the NUM had agreed to allow a number of men to help with repairs.

OLD OAKS COLLIERY, THE PROPERTY OF CHARLES CAMMELL & C° L?, CYCLOPS WORKS, SHEFFIELD.

NEW OAKS COLLIERY, THE PROPERTY OF CHARLES CAMMELL & C° L?, CYCLOPS WORKS, SHEFFIELD.

Oaks, Barnsley

The colliery was formerly the property of Messrs Firth, Bamber, and it mined a seam that was notorious for firedamp. A disaster occurred there in 1847 when seventy-three men and boys were killed. There were several explosions in a second disaster and the first took place on the 12 December 1866 when 340 people were down the mine. Only six of them survived and gave an initial death toll of 334. In addition to that twenty-seven others were killed in a succession of explosions when the workings were being explored. The final death toll was 361. The Oaks disaster remains the worst in an English coalfield. These engravings show two panoramic views of the old and new Oaks colliery.

Right: The Oaks 1866 colliery disaster monument, pictured on Doncaster Road, Barnsley, was commissioned by Samuel Joshua Cooper. It was erected 1913 and includes, on a small plinth, a bronze winged female figure in classical garb, wearing a stained bronze breastplate. She carries a wounded or dying naked man over her right shoulder as she strides forward. The man holds a broken sword in his right hand. An owl stands by the left foot of the woman. Named 'Gloria Victis', this was created by French sculptor M. J. A. Mercié, There is also a bronze plaque on the front of the pedestal.

Below: Oaks colliery No. 2 headgear pictured in July 1975. In September 1980 an NCB spokesman confirmed that as part of the development work at Barnsley Main, they had gone through into the old Oaks shafts. But they were to be permanently sealed. 'No one will ever see, or use those old shafts again,' the spokesman emphasised. And there was no question of the new workings breaking through into the Oaks workings, where a number of bodies had to be left after the 1866 disaster.

Orgreave, Sheffield

In June 1975 miners at Orgreave drove their way to a new European record carving out 222 yards of roadway in fifteen machine shifts. The achievement – equal to ten cricket pitches put end to end – was carried out by some of the team who had set up a pit record at the colliery in the previous year. Ron Windle, NUM branch secretary at the pit, said, 'The whole colliery contributed to it.' Production manager Jim Mallen said, 'It's an achievement that will take a lot of beating.' Orgreave colliery closed on 2 October 1981.

In May/June 1984 miners tried to picket the Orgreave coking plant with the intention of forcing its temporary closure. The plant turned coal into coke for use in blast furnaces. Miners' leader Arthur Scargill is seen here at Orgreave with police on 29 July 1984. He is wearing a baseball cap with the badge of the American miners' union and was worn by pitmen in Kentucky when they were in dispute with private pit owners the Amex Company. But the significance did not end there, for the Amex coal company boss at the time of the dispute was Ian McGregor.

One of the most controversial incidents of the 1984/85 strike was 'the Battle of Orgreave' which occurred on 18 June 1984. Pickets numbered between 5,000 and 6,000 and were from various parts the UK. The police had between 4,000 and 8,000 officers; many of them bussed in from other forces. Eye witnesses state there were between forty and fifty mounted police and fifty-eight police dogs. There were no female police officers and only a handful of female picketers. The picture shows an incident from a clash of 31 May 1984.

Early on 18 June 1984 pickets were escorted to a field to the north of the Orgreave plant which was surrounded on three sides by police. On the fourth side to the south was the Sheffield to Worksop railway line run. At 9.25 a.m. the fully laden lorries began to leave the coking plant and, in time, the Battle of Orgreave began with extremely ugly incidents occurring between miners and police. Records indicate that fifty-one pickets and seventy-two policemen were injured during the confrontation.

After the Battle of Orgreave approximately ninety-five pickets were charged with riot, unlawful assembly and similar offences. When a number were put on trial, all charges were dropped and lawsuits brought against the police. Eventually, South Yorkshire Police would agree to pay out approximately £425,000 in compensation and approxiamtely £100,000 in legal costs to around thirty-nine pickets in an out-of-court settlement. The picture shows police charging at Orgreave on 31 May 1984. The closure of Orgreave Coking Plant came in 1990.

Park Mill, Kirklees

'Nine miners, trapped by a roof fall, more than 600 ft down, for over two hours dug their way to freedom last night,' said the *Yorkshire Post* of 5 June 1974 in a report on an incident at Park Mill. After the miners had clawed at tons of boulders and rubble which had fallen from 11 yards of roof, they scrambled through a hole of about 18 inches and were pulled to safety by the rescue teams. The nine men were working 2½ miles from the pit bottom driving a new roadway in the Kent Fifteens Heading. Michael Eaton, the NCB North Yorkshire Area director said everyone at the colliery was intensely relieved at the outcome of the rescue response. The picture shows relatives and friends waiting at the colliery for news.

Above: In an article headed 'Pit puts on bright new face', the *Yorkshire Post* of 10 February 1987 said that the fortunes of ailing Park Mill had been turned round through a £4 million programme of investment on a new coalface and new equipment. This took it from the verge of closure to the top six of the national productivity league. Pit manager Martin Longman said the new coalface was averaging nearly 2,000 tonnes a day, three times more than the pit was producing in September of the previous year. Park Mill colliery deputies (left to right), Morris Lockwood, Brian Wood, Ken Mountain and Keith Beardsall, proudly display a car sticker proclaiming the colliery the best west of the Barnsley area.

Right:
Primrose Hill, Leeds

On 23 September 1969, the *Yorkshire Evening Post* said that these two men were fighting for the life of the colliery. They were A. Morley (left) secretary of the local branch of the NUM and 'Mick' Matthewman the branch president. Both men had worked for over thirty years at the colliery which employed over 600. The pit manager, G. Prince said that no one could guarantee the pit's future but if it closed, it would not be the fault of the men.

Left:

Prince of Wales, Wakefield

A miner at Prince of Wales, Derek Rudderham, casts his vote in a National ballot, which was held at the colliery on 8 March 1983. He is watched by his workmates, John Appleton and Mick Tomlin. The ballot called for a national strike to support the action of Welsh miners against the closure of Lewis Merthyr colliery but was defeated. The ballot result was 76,540 voting 'yes' in favour of a strike and 118,954 voting 'no' against a strike (39 per cent for, 61 per cent against). Yorkshire voted 27,597 for and 23,841 against; South Wales voted 11,800 for and 5,500 against.

Below: Despite failing to prevent the National Coal Board (NCB) implementing its programme of pit closures, many strikers marched back to work defiantly, with union banners flying and bands playing on 5 March 1985. Prince of Wales miners are seen on that date.

Miner Chris Owen sits in the locker room at the Prince of Wales, following his final shift underground on Friday 30 August, 2002. Some of the 450 miners who used to work at the pit marked the closure with a small ceremony.

Prince of Wales closed in December 1980 but mining was not to end. Men were transferred to the Prince of Wales drift mine which was opened earlier in that year at a cost of £50 million by Prince Charles. In August 1992, the colliery produced 50,000 tonnes of coal in a week. Colliery manager Dick Davies said, 'The Prince is responding magnificently to the challenges thrown down to British Coal to cut costs and improve productivity.' Ten years later the colliery closed.

Above:

Ricall, Selby

The *Yorkshire Evening Post* of 13 November 1980 said that heavyweight lifting at Ricall was to be undertaken by a Caruthers goliath overhead gantry crane. An identical crane to the one at Ricall (pictured), able to lift loads of up to 20 tonnes, over a 30-metre span, was also being installed at Stillingfleet.

Left: A new landmark grew at Ricall in January 1994. A concrete structure for the 98-ft upcast winder tower was cast in eleven days. The building work was the responsibility of Fairclough Building. It was designed jointly between Fletcher Ross & Hickling, the Leeds architects and W. S. Atkin & Partners, the Birmingham engineers. This new mine at Ricall was the third of the five Selby pits.

In December 1984, coal was cut for the first time since the strike at Ricall. The *Yorkshire Post* reported on 13 December that forty-nine miners, including one deputy – about a fifth of the normal workforce – were expected to produce between 100 and 200 tonnes a day. The miners, many of whom had been reporting to work for several weeks, were brought to and from the pit for day shifts by buses under police escort. An NUM spokesman said, 'Obviously this is designed to have a psychological effect on the lads still on strike but they have tried that so often we don't take any notice any more.' Ricall colliery closed in 2004.

Rothwell, Leeds

Miners picketing Rothwell scored a victory early on 9 February 1972 when safety men on the night shift gave up their attempts to get into the pit. When the deputies arrived on the road leading to the colliery, they were faced by a corridor of angry miners through which they would have had to pass. Despite the strong police contingent on hand to escort them, the deputies decided to retreat. The delighted miners pictured here, many of whom had been on picket duty for twenty-four hours or more, cheered.

Royston Drift, Barnsley

Members of the UL 24 face team which produced 2,500 tonnes of coal in a shift at Royston in September 1980. The picture shows team members Ernest Whitehouse, Jim Oldham, George Marshall, Alan Wilkinson, Terry Tuite, Ray Carter, Alan Bowman, George Crummack, Dave Smith, Ken Shepherd, Walter Oliver, Fred Hanson, Mike Holbrooke, Dave Allen and manager Neil Kemp.

Miners at Royston Drift had their own 'underground' train service to take them to and from the coalface. The picture dates from September 1983.

Five

Savile to Treeton

Savile, Leeds

View of the colliery, 18 September 1963. Two 14-ft-diameter shafts were sunk to the Haigh Moor seam in 1874, and they were 143 yards deep. A list (from the Coal Mining History Resource Centre) for 1880 shows a massive 111 collieries in Leeds. On www.methley-village.com it is mentioned that the upcast shaft was deepened to the Beeston seam in 1909 to act as an upcast shaft for the neighbouring Silkstone and Beeston workings of Whitwood colliery on the Methley side. After the closure of Whitwood the shaft was part filled to the Flockton horizon in 1970. Between the years 1956 and 1958 major reconstruction took place.

Left: During September 1963 a group of miners staged a sit down strike at Savile pit bottom. They had been demanding extra pay for working a difficult coalface and came up after three days when the management agreed to discuss their grievance. This stock picture of Savile was intended to feature in a *Yorkshire Post* article of 22 December 1977 titled 'Yorks Pits Defy Scargill on Bonuses'. But it was not used. The article stated that the NCB had listed fifteen Yorkshire pits where incentive productivity deals were being negotiated in defiance of the Yorkshire miner's leader. In the following month there was to be a ballot on the issue. The view shows men leaving the cage at the pit-top.

Below: Savile colliery entrance, 8 March 1984. The colliery closed in 1985.

Sharlston, Wakefield

'The miners' strike is having a telling effect on Sharlston,' wrote the *Yorkshire Evening Post* on 29 October 1984. Families were breaking up. Some wives were returning to their parents and taking their children with them. The fight to survive was becoming desperate. At the weekly share of food parcels in the miners welfare, 400 men and women turned up to accept the parcel provided by the union – eight items to a bag, usually a few tins, biscuits, a packet of tea. But on one occasion there were only 290 parcels available. More than 100 families were turned away empty-handed, to scour for food elsewhere. Striking miners are pictured queuing for food parcels at Sharlton Miners' Welfare.

Charlie Livingstone, an ex-paratrooper twice blown up in Northern Ireland, was a striking miner in October 1984 with a wife and two children to support. But the guitar with which he passed idle hours during his shifts off-duty in Belfast was being put to use at social evenings, concerts and other fund-raising events to raise cash to help feeding the people of Sharlston. When standing on street corners collecting in non-mining communities he received taunts. But for every jibe there were a dozen people who made a contribution.

Inset: The swinging sound of a 1940s style big band put miners at Sharlston 'in the mood' when they emerged from their shift underground on 9 February 1989. The men are pictured left after reaching the pit-top to find the Little Big Band holding an impromptu rehearsal in the colliery yard for their appearance in a show 'Miller and Me', which was staged at Wakefield Theatre Royal & Opera House. The show, written by Paul Bond with music composed by conductor Patrick Dailey (pictured), was staged to coincide with the fiftieth anniversary of the Blitz in Britain for Panacea Productions.

Above: A 140-ft chimney at Sharlston collapsed as demolition expert 'Blaster' Bates detonated nearly 20 lb of explosives in November 1985. The chimney was built in the early 1940s to replace two other chimneys used in conjunction with a coal-fired boiler plant on the pit-top, providing steam for winding and for heating. An NCB spokesman said electricity had replaced the coal boiler at the pit a year earlier and the chimney was no longer required.

The *Yorkshire Post* of 29 May 1993 stated that the last full shift ended at Sharlston on the previous day. With the exception of a few salvage workers dismantling machinery beneath the pit village, most of the 535 miners walked out of the colliery gates for the last time. They were angry and bitter towards a government they felt hard turned its back on the industry. About 150 miners were offered a transfer to Selby but the rest had taken redundancy. 'Many of the men leaving their last shift were too upset to stop and talk,' said the *Yorkshire Post*. The picture shows miners coming up from Sharlston for the last time.

Sharlston pictured on the day of closure 28 May 1993.

Left: On 9 July 1993 Sharlston miners laid a wreath for all their colleagues who had died underground at the doomed pit.

Below: On 9 July 1993, Sharlston miners staged a last march through the village with the pit banner.

Opposite above: In January 1994 more than 2,000 people voiced their objection over plans for an opencast mine in the shadow of Sharlston colliery which had closed some months earlier. A petition, signed by almost all the residents of Sharlston and New Sharlston and backed by neighbouring villagers at Warmfield, Crofton, Streethouse and Heath, was handed to the Mayor of Wakefield, Cllr Horace Clark. But plans to extract shallow-laying coal, fireclay and red shale from the site as part of a self-financing reclamation scheme were approved by Wakefield Council. In recent years the derelict site has been redeveloped.

Silverwood, Rotherham

Shortly after 8 a.m. on 3 February 1966 forty miners boarded a paddy train to begin their shift at Silverwood. The journey was mainly a downhill run and following behind was a second train known as the mail train, carrying equipment. The mail train suddenly lost control, picking up speed until it caught up with the train in front, smashing into the rear. Nine men died instantly, one man survived a further three days in hospital and thirty miners were injured. In a report on the accident by the Mines Inspectorate a point was made that in future, a train carrying materials must not follow a man-riding train. Casualties pictured after treatment at Rotherham Doncaster Gate hospital are l to r: Leslie France, Luke Brennan, John Hallsworth and Ernest Devine.

Pictured are three of the nursing sisters who went underground to give aid to the injured (left to right): Sister Kathleen Payne, Sister Dianne Adsetts and Sister Mary Parton. Sister Adsetts said the scene of the crash was 'just a shambles. There were so many injured it was hard to decide who needed treatment first.' One of the men she attended had both his legs amputated. After all the injured and dead had been brought to the surface, Sister Adsetts went round with another Coal Board employee to inform relatives of those who had died at the pit. Sister Adsetts was employed at Silverwood.

Silverwood was sunk by the Dalton Mining Company between April 1900 and December 1903. Two shafts, both sunk to the south of Hollings Lane, entered the Barnsley Seam at a depth of 750 yards. The Barnsley seam provided most of the output at Silverwood until the Melton field was developed in 1952. Large housing estates were built to cater for the flow of miners into the area in Thrybergh, Bramley, Dalton, Wickersley, the garden village of Sunnyside, and Ravenfield Common. Miners at Silverwood are seen waiting to go underground, 8 February 1967.

Above and below: The Queen went down Silverwood colliery on 30 July 1975. She was shadowed by Mrs Ivy Foulkes, the colliery's nursing officer, throughout the ninety minutes spent underground. 'I took equipment down in case she fainted or anything else happened but everything went smoothly,' Ivy said. The Queen mined a lump of coal herself, then hewed a piece at the coalface and carried it back to the pit-top. On the surface she showed her souvenir to Ronald Gray, a face worker, and Alan Ibbotson, a machine operator, who were waiting to go down on the afternoon shift. Ronald said the Queen told them, 'I have actually hewn a piece myself.' She added that the visit was 'quite an experience.' In the pit, the Queen unveiled a plaque commemorating the Royal visit. She was accompanied by the Duke of Edinburgh who was surprised to learn that pit ponies had been used as recently as 1971 at Silverwood. The seam he and the Queen visited was 600 yards underground and 1¾ miles from the pit bottom.

At one time Silverwood adopted Tina Turner's song 'Simply the Best' because of continually smashing the country's productivity figures and claiming to mine the world's cheapest coal. Tina herself commented, 'I'm proud to be associated with these guys.' But even record-breaking figures could not save the pit, which at the height of production employed approximately 3,000 men. The workforce dwindled from 790 on 1992 to 200 at the beginning of 1994. The last shift is seen leaving Silverwood on 23 December 1994. NUM branch secretary, Granville Richardson said, 'It's going to be a sad Christmas. But the men have been under such mental pressure since the closure announcement they are relieved to know the end has finally come.'

South Kirkby, Wakefield

Sinking operations in the South Kirkby area were begun by the Ferryhill and Rosedale Iron Company and the main target was the Barnsley seam, which was reached at a depth of 635 yards in August 1878. Disappointingly, the owners ran out of cash and, with increasing liabilities, stopped all work in 1879. A new limited company, with John Shaw of Darrington Hall as chairman, took over in 1880, and work progressed to open out both the Barnsley Bed and the Haigh Moor Seams. The picture shows pit ponies underground at South Kirkby in January 1968.

Above: Arthur Scargill at South Kirkby, *c.* 1980.
Born on 11 January 1938, Arthur was President of
the Yorkshire branch of the NUM from 1973 until
1981 and National President of the union from
1982 to 2002.

Right: At the outset of the 1984/85 miners strike,
it was claimed that South Kirkby was a potential
time bomb as dangerous methane gas built up. On
11 March 1984 pickets were on duty at the pit
– seen here – when a team of managers arrived to
keep watch on the fans and pumps. A management
spokesman said pickets began dictating how many
of the managers could go down the pit. 'In our
opinion we required twice the number of managers
that the pickets said they were prepared to allow,'
he added. The *Yorkshire Post* of 12 March alleged
that no-one from the NUM was available to
comment.

On www.mike-duffy.me.uk/south_kirkby_colliery it is mentioned that the Beamshaw Seam was developed at South Kirkby and, in 1958, a third shaft was sunk at the pit to allow further development of coal in places like the Newhill Seam. At its peak, South Kirkby employed almost 3,000 men, and in the 60s and 70s produced over one million tons of coal in a financial year to earn the nickname 'Big SK'. 'Some of the seams by-passed initially were worked by the creation of the Ferrymoor-Riddings Drift Mine, which opened in the '70s, and used retreat mining. They were united into a complex with a washery, although the workforce had dropped to around 1,100 by the time of the miners' strike in 1984.' South Kirkby colliery is pictured on 14 November 1988.

On 23 August 1935, ten men were killed at South Kirkby in an explosion. Details are given on www.cmhrc.co.uk: 'Several men were building stoppings to seal off a area in the Barnsley Seam where there had been an explosion of firedamp when there was an explosion within the sealed off area. Rescue operations were started at once when there was a further explosion at 5.50pm which burned the party carrying out the last casualty Frank Dale. 10 killed and 2 injured in first explosion and 5 injured in second.' The picture shows a miner underground at South Kirkby which closed in 1988.

Right and below: South Kirkby and Moorthorpe Town Council are seen at the unveiling ceremony of a sculpture by Graham Ibbeson on 27 November 2005. It is dedicated to the memory of all the miners of Kirkby and Frickley collieries who lost their lives in the mines. From left, Thomas Allsopp, Mayor of South Kirkby and Moorthorpe Town Council, Jon Trickett MP Hemsworth, Coun Peter Box, Leader City of Wakefield Metropolitan District Council, Graham Ibbeson, sculptor, and Laurie Harrison, Leader South Kirkby and Moorthorpe Town Council.

St John's, Normanton

In May 1975 the Yorkshire NUM council delegates decided to call off the threatened coalfield strike over the NCB's plans to close the approximately 600-man St John's, despite feelings that they had 'a good case'. The decision was taken at the council meeting at Barnsley after delegates heard that the pit, had agreed to accept the board's decision to close it. St John's colliery was once suggested as the location for the National Mining Museum and is pictured here on 10 March 1973. It had been in existence since *c*. 1870 and three men were killed in an explosion at colliery on 26 September, 1959.

Stillingfleet, Selby

Stillingfleet colliery underground repair work 4 June 1985.

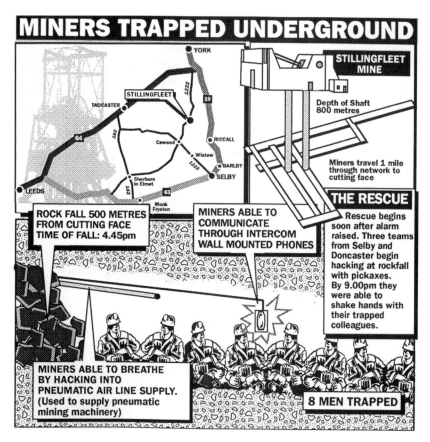

Eight miners were trapped half a mile underground when the tunnel they were working on collapsed behind them on 6 April 1992. The eight – six miners, a pit deputy and a mining engineer – were operating a tunnelling machine under Stillingfleet mine. After about three hours the rescuers had excavated a hole large enough for them to be able to shake hands with their trapped colleagues and pass them turkey and corned beef sandwiches and cartons of orange juice. This graphic which appeared in the *Yorkshire Post* of 7 April, illustrates the event.

A miner at Stillingfleet pictured as he finished a shift in November 1997. The picture was taken to illustrate a *Yorkshire Post* article detailing a contract where RJB mining would supply National Power with 18 million tonnes of coal over a three-year period. But, the picture was not used.

Temple Newsam, Leeds

This picture appeared on the front page of the *Yorkshire Post* on 11 September 1975 and illustrated an article headed 'Mining threat to last barrier'. The article stated that the Coal Board planned to extend open-cast mining at Temple Newsam and that could mean the destruction of the last barrier of trees, seen on the left, between the existing open-cast site and the façade of the mansion.

During March 1974, two attempts to pull down a coal pulverising shed at the Oxbow open-cast mine at Temple Newsam ended in failure, said the *Yorkshire Post* on Monday 1 April 1974. The 50-ft-high building acquired a 20 degree list during the previous week when the army had tried to blow it up. A few days later, they were back again to pull it down – but without any further success. Members of 272 Field Support Squadron, Royal Engineers Volunteers, used steel ropes attached to bulldozers to try and topple the building. '[But] the bulldozers were not big enough for the job – and so the saga continues for a few more days at least,' said the newspaper.

On 23 February 1994 the *Yorkshire Evening Post* said it was campaigning vigorously for checks to be placed on the spread of open-cast mining across Yorkshire's green field sites – many of them within a stone's throw of the country's deep-mined pits. The picture above illustrated an article on the subject and was intended to show the devastation caused by open-cast mining to the countryside around Temple Newsam.

Thorne, Doncaster

'Thorne Colliery, closed for the previous 11 years whilst flood prevention work costing £1.6 m was carried out, is still shut,' said the *Yorkshire Post* of 28 November 1967. More than 2,000 men had to travel to other pits when the colliery closed and many were still travelling. They were deployed to Hickleton, Hatfield, Armthorpe, Rossington, Askern, Bullcroft, Bentley and Brodsworth. The most distant colliery – Hickleton – was 22 miles away which added about two hours to the men's working day.

In January 1968, Thorne had the highest unemployment figure of any town in the Yorkshire and Humberside region – 9.2 per cent. 'So the announcement by the Coal Board that mining will not be resumed at the colliery, came as a bombshell,' said the *Yorkshire Post* of 8 January in an article headed 'Men of Thorne Bitter at Pit Closure'. County Ald. G. H. Nicholson who started work there in 1926, said, 'There's more than 100 years of coal-getting at Thorne colliery. It's the finest house coal in the country, with the smallest ash content and it goes right out to the North Sea.'

Thornhill, Dewsbury

In 1893, the Combs pit, Thornhill, mining disaster killed 139 miners. Seven were rescued and they are pictured here. On www.healeyhero.co.uk it is mentioned that 'at the time of the explosion the Combs Pit was being worked by a single shift. The men went down at 6 a.m. and returned to the surface at 2 p.m. each day. On the day of the explosion there were 146 people in the mine including the under-manager, two deputies and fifty seven boys.' The explosion took place a few minutes after midday during the men's dinner hour. Thornhill colliery resulted from the merging of Inghams and Combs colliery in 1948 but closed in 1971.

Thurcroft, Rotherham

The main shafts at the colliery were sunk by Rotherhvale Collieries Ltd between 1909 and 1912; the Barnsley seam being reached in 1913 and exploited until 1968. Other seams mined are as follows: Park Gate (1942–74); Haigh Moor (1971–91); Swallow Wood (1983–91). The colliery closed in November 1991 leaving many thousands of tons of workable coal underground. The photograph was taken on 4 September 1991.

A campaign to reopen the mine was begun shortly after closure with redundant miners forming Thurcroft 92 Ltd. The two people depicted in June 1992 are: Paul Roddis, NUM rep (left), and Chris Mallender from Rotherham Council who was helping to organise the pit buy. C. Mallender is holding a campaign booklet that was produced to hand out to interested ex-miners.

At the beginning of October 1992 workmen sealed the fate of the Thurcroft mining dream. Thousands of tonnes of concrete were poured into the abandoned workings of the pit, ending forever the hope that the pit could be reopened as a workers' co-operative. As work began, Chris Mallander, the man who led Rotherham Borough Council's efforts to help the miners, condemned British Coal and the Government for destroying the pit. 'It is costing hundreds of thousands of pounds to fill in the pit, and in doing so, millions of pounds of equipment and reserves are being lost forever,' he said. Contractors are seen stripping the pit shaft on 29 July 1992.

Treeton, Rotherham

On 26 April 1967 tempers became hot when the bath water turned cold at Treeton. Coal-blackened miners threatened strike action when they surfaced after eight hours underground to find the bath water was icy cold, because of a boiler fault. Nightshift miners went home still caked in coal dust. In the bathhouse at the pithead groups of disgruntled men had gathered in protest. But later the annoyance was calmed. Union officials had accepted steps taken by colliery engineers to get the hot water flowing again. This picture accompanied the article about the incident. Sinking of the Treeton colliery shafts began in 1875 but work was suspended in September 1878 then resumed in March 1882. The colliery ceased production on Wednesday 5 December 1990.

Six

Walton to Yorkshire Main

Walton, Wakefield

Mine rescue teams from Walton and Rothwell, who were involved in the Lofthouse colliery disaster, gave underwater demonstrations at the reservoir at Walton in July 1975. The teams are shown with a stretcher under the supervision of Mr John Dawes, assistant supervisor at Wakefield Mines Rescue Station. The exercise was a result of the disaster.

Water Haigh, Leeds

The colliery is pictured during a strike by the Yorkshire Winding Engine Men's Association on 8 January 1964. The *Yorkshire Post* of that date reported that although only 560 strong, association members were key personnel responsible for winding men and materials in the shafts of more than ninety of Yorkshire's 103 collieries. The Association had begun a series of weekly token stoppages because the Coal Board would not recognise it as a negotiating body. Running concurrently with that issue was a problem over the inability of the YWEMA and the Yorkshire Area NUM to agree to terms for merging.

On 14 October 1969 police cars drove into the yard of Water Haigh, before strike pickets met some of the 139 men still producing coal at the pit. All the other seventy-four pits in the Yorkshire coalfields were still on strike – the second day of the stoppage over surface worker hours. An angry meeting of over 300 of the 600 Water Haigh men had decided to tackle colleagues who were still working.

Wath, Rotherham

Wath was sunk by the Wath Main Colliery Co. Ltd, reaching the Barnsley seam in 1876. The shafts were deepened in 1912 and 1923 and the following seams were worked: Barnsley, Parkgate, High Moor and Melton. The 1923 *Colliery Year Book and Coal Trades Directory* records that the annual output of coal in that year was 600,000 tons. The number of men employed underground was 1,823 and above ground 546. The class of coal was coking, gas, household and steam. Seven miners were killed in an explosion at the colliery on 24 February 1930.

Wath Main eventually became part of the Manvers complex and closed on 23 January 1987 with, it was alleged, a year's coal still underground. The closure was prompted in November of the previous year when men voted in a secret ballot in favour of the action. In March 2000 the giant Manvers Regeneration Scheme at Wath won a major award. The area shared the Civic Trust's Top Landscape Award with Sheffield's Heart of the City Project. Hundreds of acres of land – formerly the site of Wath colliery and the Manvers Coking Plant were reclaimed.

West Riding, Wakefield

'By the end of the year the pit that has been a way of life for the village of Altofts, for over a century will have yielded its last ton of coal,' reported the *Yorkshire Evening Post* of 1 June 1963; adding, 'West Riding colliery's reserves are nearly exhausted.' The labour force was run down from 1200 in 1958 to 400 in 1963 and West Riding or 'Pope's' as they called it at Altofts – a nickname derived from the private owners Pope & Pearson – was soon to be handed over to the salvage men. There was no shock, no surprise, in the long rows of miners' cottages. Miners didn't need official statements to tell them that the seams that provided a livelihood for themselves, their fathers and their grandfathers were running out. For some men the closure meant special problems. West Riding's horse-keeper, sixty-year-old Thomas Hobson would be parted from the animals he had worked with for years. He said, 'There's old Tom out of the Flockton seam – he's 37. What will happen to him? And Randy. He's my favourite. I wonder if they'll let me keep him – ah, well probably not.'

Wharncliffe Silkstone, Barnsley

A postcard showing Wharncliffe Silkstone colliery near Barnsley and the eleven men killed in the explosion on 30 May 1914.

Wharncliffe Woodmoor, Barnsley

On 16 October 1979 Yorkshire NUM president Arthur Scargill unveils a memorial to fifty-eight men who died in a pit disaster on 6 August 1936 at Wharncliffe Woodmoor colliery. Made from pithead winding gear, the memorial was placed on the reclaimed site of the former colliery at Carlton near Barnsley. Harry Dancer, Chairman of Barnsley MBC's Development and Planning Committee, initiated this scheme which was accepted by that committee on 31 August 1978 and cost £950, approved on 29 September 1978. Barnsley's MP, Roy Mason, third from right was among the onlookers. Arthur Scargill said the memorial should remind everyone of the price of coal and the debt owed to the mining industry. In 2008 Barnsley Councillor Len Picken (Councillor Picken was the Mayor of Barnsley for the municipal year 2007/2008) successfully campaigned to have the old half pulley wheel moved to a more prominent location at the entrance of the Wharncliff Business Park. The new memorial was a more emotive piece of work that included the half pulley wheel, a stone frieze, sculptured by Harry Malkin, carved in brick supplied and fired by the Ibstock Brick Co., Wakefield, that depicts two miners searching for their lost colleagues and stands about 10 feet by 8. It also includes local news reports from the time of the accident, an information board and the names of the Woodmoor victims. The ceremony was led by Councillor Picken and Councillor Roy Butterfield. More than 100 people attended, including numerous relatives and descendants, some with Welsh origins, and representatives from the NUM. The colliery closed in 1966 as a result of the NCB's pit closure programme.

Wheldale, Castleford

Opened in 1868, Castleford's Wheldale colliery became a scene of confrontation on 20 November 1984 as frustrated pickets renewed their struggle to save the strike at the pit. The picture shows police in riot gear near a smashed street lamp. The colliery closed in 1987.

Wheldale miners leave the cage on 19 October 1987. On www.wakefield.gov.uk it is mentioned that the former Fryston and Wheldale colliery sites have been successfully transformed into country trails. The site now offers over 8 km of footpaths, bridleways and carriageway and other educational and learning opportunities including an outdoor classroom and river wharf facility. An £8 million remediation programme was put into place plus investment in the village from the National Coalfield Programme.

Right: Cherry trees have been planted at a defunct Castleford colliery to help commemorate miners killed at the pit or while serving in the Second World War, said the *Yorkshire Evening Post* of 26 April 1994. The facelift for the Wheldale colliery memorial was part of a rejuvenation project for almost 250 acres of spoil heap and derelict land at the mine and its neighbour Fryston colliery. Wakefield council was spending £18,000 restoring the ironwork of the memorial – made by pit craftsmen – and on landscaping the surroundings. Cllr Gerard Byrne, Chairman of Fryston Wheldale Liaison Committee is pictured with the re-sited Wheldale Memorial.

Below: The *Yorkshire Evening Post* of 2 May 1989 said, 'Castleford's once glorious mining industry has come one step closer to oblivion now the demolition of surface buildings at Wheldale has begun.' Though virtually all installations at the pit were to disappear in weeks, it would not vanish completely for at least another two years. A grimy gantry which carried electricity cables across Wheldon Road would be left intact, because power was needed to scavenge thousands of tons of 'carpet coal' left over from Wheldale's years of existence.

Whitemoor, Selby

A pre-erected mineshaft head-frame being lifted into position at Whitemoor by Qualter Hall
& Co. Ltd; the main shaft equipment contractor. The picture illustrated an article in a mining
industry review in the *Yorkshire Post* on 26 September 1986. Qualter Hall's general sales manager
said that constant involvement in such projects as Selby and the need to continuously update shaft
facilities at other long life mines enabled such companies as his own to stay in the forefront of
technology and use the experience to good effect in other mining projects at home and abroad.

On 18 April 1985, the *Yorkshire Post* reported that the latest milestone in the Selby coalfield was the installation of the permanent headgear over the No. 2 shaft at Whitemoor. The 100-tonne steel frame made by Qualter Hall of Barnsley was hoisted into place in a two-minute lift, and the winding wheels followed. 'The complete structure will be enclosed in stone-faced blockwork and the wheels will resolve unseen,' said the *Yorkshire Post*; adding, 'Underground tunnelling is establishing a pit bottom circuit, and driving towards the neighbouring Ricall mine, a mile away.'

A strike over bonus payments by 3,000 miners brought the Selby coalfield to a standstill in February 1987. Union leader Ken Capstick said, '[Management] have confiscated our bonus pay and we consider it theft.' Management argued that the dispute was not over that issue but because miners had taken a certain dislike to various officials, including an MP, visiting their pits. Whitemoor pickets are seen here on 16 February after stopping pit deputies from going to work. Union leaders in the Selby coalfield said their strike would cost British Coal about £1.5 million in lost production. British Coal said the stoppage would cost the 3,000 miners about £750,000 in pay.

Above: Energy Minister Tim Eggar, second from right, emerges from an underground tour of Whitemoor on 17 July 1992. Pictured with him (from left), Phillip Gwilliam, Selby MP Michael Alison, and Selby Coalfield director Alan Houghton. Tim Eggar spent two hours underground accompanied by British Coal deputy chairman Albert Wheeler. Later, he opened the Dinnington Business Centre, near Rotherham, on behalf of British Coal Enterprise which helped to find jobs for redundant pit workers.

Opposite below:

Whitwood, Wakefield

Early sinking operations at the colliery are given on www.dmm-pitwork.org.uk: 'The two shafts were sunk between 1871–78 and are situated about 2 ½ miles west of that point at which coal measures dip under the Permian. The Beeston shaft, a downcast, is sunk to a depth of 501 yards and is 14 ft. in diameter. This shaft was not sunk beyond the Silkstone Seam until 1914 ...' The colliery's owner Henry Briggs of Henry Briggs, Son & Company Ltd employed a profit-sharing scheme for his workers. He also commissioned internationally recognised architect Charles F. A. Voysey, to design housing – Whitwood Terrace – and a Miners' Institute for his workforce. The pit finally closed around March 1968.

Above left:

Wistow, Selby

In April 1979, Bill Forrest, Deputy Director (Mining) in the NCB's North Yorkshire Area, takes a measuring rod to the fully exposed Barnsley seam which checked out at 2.7 metres (8 ft 10 in) in thickness at Wistow. Bill Forrest had piloted the Selby Project from its inception and at that time the entry into the seam by the No.1 shaft at Wistow was a major landmark in the scheme's progress. With Bill Forrest is Wistow's mine deputy, Joe Willoughby.

Above right: Pictured at the Wistow 'topping out' on 23 October 1981 are NCB Selby chief Trevor Massey and McAlpine Project Director Jim Lord.

'The coal starts to flow at Selby,' said the *Yorkshire Post* of 23 September 1983. 'Wistow's A1 coalface became operational on Monday July 4, and this steel cord belt in the drift mine's South Tunnel was commissioned on time to carry the first output.'

'NCB claims that miners at Wistow wanted to return to work were described as "total rubbish" by pickets on duty there today,' said the *Yorkshire Evening Post* of 8 May 1984. The pickets outside the pit at 6.30 a.m. when the main shift would normally begin said they knew nothing of the claims. One of the miners said, 'If there had been any talk of men going back to work here there would have been 1,000 pickets at the entrance today.' Another miner said, 'No miners have been through the picket line and we don't know of any that want to.' Pickets were allowing management through as usual and the number of miners on the picket lines was being kept to a minimum. The *Yorkshire Evening Post* caption beneath the picture here, read, 'Lonely vigil for the pickets at Wistow ... as the man the gateway in the early hours. A blazing brazier keeps away the morning chill.'

In the week beginning 20 July 1987 miners at Wistow smashed the British output and productivity records. The pit's 900 men produced 67,104 tonnes bettering a national record by nearly 1,000 tonnes. They are pictured celebrating their success with National coal queen, Miss Andrea Davies, twenty-one. The record made production levels at the mine amongst the best in the world. Colliery manager, Eric Wilby said, 'When the miners realised they were on course for a record, every shift worked flat out to make sure they made it.'

Eastenders star Anita Dobson is given a lift by pools' winners at Wistow on 6 July 1988 after presenting them with a cheque for £891,000. From left they are: Kerry Austin, David Hinchcliffe, Bernard Aldred, Ron Wainwright, and Ron Howe. The five friends started their syndicate in 1984, each contributing £1.10 but had to give up during the miners' strike. Ron Howe started the group but handed over to Ron Wainwright after the pit dispute. The cheque was presented at the Yorkshire Mining Museum at Caphouse colliery.

Miners at Wistow celebrate with a toast in beer on 19 January 1993 after smashing three European coal-mining records. The men at Wistow sank their pithead pints to mark a record weekly output tonnage of 173,156 tonnes. They also hit the Euro best of 100,000 tonnes from one coalface in a week and became the first British mine to produce 2 million tonnes since the start of the financial year – the fastest in Europe. In recognition of the productivity hat-trick, management set up a bar on a service road outside the pit rescue room and miners toasted their success.

A miner carries a symbolic piece of coal after finishing his final shift at Wistow on 13 May 2004. UK coal said that in previous weeks miners at the last of the 130 faces to be worked at Wistow since production began twenty-one years earlier had to contend with geological faulting, roof falls, and inflows of water. Of the 120 miners left at Wistow, forty were to be made redundant. Another forty would transfer to the remaining Selby mines and the remaining forty would stay at Wistow to salvage equipment for other UK Coal mines. The NUM said it was a 'very sad' day for the coal industry.

Hundreds of tons of concrete and steel came crashing down at Wistow on 1 July 2005 as demolition contractors blew up the winding tower at the derelict mine. Contracts manager Paul Bloom said the demolition, which took more than a week to prepare, had gone smoothly, despite the close proximity of other buildings only 15 ft from the tower which was 88 ft high and 30 ft across. Contractors were planning to crush the concrete and salvage the steel for scrap before demolishing other buildings on the site. That was expected to take a further three months.

Woolley, Barnsley/ Wakefield

In 1963 four miners at Woolley pose with Monarch the pit pony and his carer or pony boy Eric Humphrey (second from the right). In 1913 there were 70,000 pit ponies at work in Britain, according to the Government Digest of Statistics. When the NCB was formed in 1947 it inherited 21,000 pit ponies, but by 1952 the total number of working ponies was down to 15,500 and, by 1973, 490.

General view of Woolley, where NUM leader Arthur Scargill started work aged fifteen in 1953.

This picture illustrated a *Yorkshire Post* article of 24 September 1982 headed 'Investment aids recovery'. It was part a supplement titled 'Coal Mining, the 1982 Review', which announced that Barnsley was undergoing a renaissance. John Keirs, the Coal Board's Director for Barnsley said that capital spending was running at around £2 million a week and the most dramatic and apparent development was the concentration of removing coal from the area's eighteen pits to just three centres at Woolley colliery (adjacent to the M1), at Grimethorpe and at South Kirkby.

Police lines at Woolley in October 1984.

The *Yorkshire Evening Post* of 3 October 1984 alleged that three police officers were injured in scuffles with 1,000 miners outside Woolley colliery earlier that day. The trouble flared as a lone working miner was escorted to the pit by police. Burning barricades were set up by pickets and police came under a barrage of stones. Material from a dry stone wall and other rubble was used in a bid to block the approach road. A police spokeswoman said she had no reports of any arrest or any serious injuries amongst the picketing miners. A police inspector was taken to hospital with a suspected broken ankle suffered when pickets were said to have pushed forward against the police line. Several days after this incident the lone rebel miner, who was the first to return to work in the Barnsley area since the 'back to work movement' began, was attacked. Initially after working for a day, he had been persuaded to stay away. But changed his mind and continued to work. He was taken to Barnsley General Hospital for treatment, but later discharged.

Woolley merged with North Gawber shortly after the 1984/85 strike and closed on 22 December 1987. Miners at the pit voted to end the fight against closure after British Coal offered every man a £5,000 redundancy bonus if shutdown was accepted by Christmas – a move which the NUM scathingly branded as blackmail. Claims were also made that the industry was being trimmed down to present an attractive package for privatising. Woolley washery plant is seen just prior to demolition on 21 February 1993.

For a time on 21 February 1993 the M1 near Barnsley was closed as the former Woolley 'washery' was demolished by a controlled explosion. Later in the year traffic was stopped again when the coal preparation plant came crashing to the ground.

Yorkshire Main (Edlington), Doncaster

Yorkshire Main was situated in the parish of Edlington. The sinking was commenced in December 1909 and completed in July 1911. The colliery's fire brigade is proudly posing here in the pit yard. Amongst those identified are Jos Gawthorpe (under-manager), Lawrie Beardsley, Johnny Walker (manager). The buildings in the background include the engine house, blacksmith's shop and boiler.

The picture shows Yorkshire Main brass band in the pit yard c. 1930.

'A derelict colliery site being transformed into homes and shops is to have a permanent memorial to its heritage,' said the *Yorkshire Post* of 23 May 1991. Part of the former Yorkshire Main colliery's pithead winding gear was, on the previous day, winched into its new home at the development site in Edlington, near Doncaster. The 42-acre Yorkshire Main site was being transformed in a £25 million scheme by the local developers, Yorkshire Metropolitan Properties. Half of the wheel was to be built into a memorial to the site's history. The pit was one of the first casualties after the 1984/85 miners' strike. It closed in October 1985.

Miners at Yorkshire Main proudly march back to work in March 1985.